www.hants.gov.uk/library

Hampshire
County Council

Love YOUR LIBRARY

Tel: 0300 555 1387

In This Book

QuickStart Guide

Your keys to understanding the city – we help you decide what to do and how to do it

Need to Know
Tips for a smooth trip

Neighbourhoods
What's where

Explore Vienna

The best things to see and do, neighbourhood by neighbourhood

Top Sights
Make the most of your visit

Local Life
The insider's city

The Best of Vienna

The city's highlights in handy lists to help you plan

Best Walks
See the city on foot

Vienna's Best...
The best experiences

Survival Guide

Tips and tricks for a seamless, hassle-free city experience

Getting Around
Travel like a local

Essential Information
Including where to stay

Our selection of the city's best places to eat, drink and experience:

◎ **Sights**

✖ **Eating**

🍷 **Drinking**

✪ **Entertainment**

🛍 **Shopping**

These symbols give you the vital information for each listing:

☎ Telephone Numbers		👪	Family-Friendly
⊙ Opening Hours		🐾	Pet-Friendly
P Parking		🚌	Bus
⊖ Nonsmoking		⛴	Ferry
@ Internet Access		Ⓜ	Metro
🛜 Wi-Fi Access		Ⓢ	Subway
🥗 Vegetarian Selection		🚋	Tram
📖 English-Language Menu		🚃	Train

Find each listing quickly on maps for each neighbourhood:

Bar Hemingway

16 🍷 Map p233, B2

Legend has it that Hemi
self, wielding a machine
...rate this timber-pan
...ered bar during
...showpiece is a
...en by Papa ar
...town. Dress
...s.com; Hôtel Rit
...⊙6.30pm-2a

Lonely Planet's Vienna

Lonely Planet Pocket Guides are designed to get you straight to the heart of the city.

Inside you'll find all the must-see sights, plus tips to make your visit to each one really memorable. We've split the city into easy-to-navigate neighbourhoods and provided clear maps so you'll find your way around with ease. Our expert authors have searched out the best of the city: walks, food, nightlife and shopping, to name a few. Because you want to explore, our 'Local Life' pages will take you to some of the most exciting areas to experience the real Vienna.

And of course you'll find all the practical tips you need for a smooth trip: itineraries for short visits; how to get around, and how much to tip the guy who serves you a drink at the end of a long day's exploration.

It's your guarantee of a really great experience.

Our Promise

You can trust our travel information because Lonely Planet authors visit the places we write about, each and every edition. We never accept freebies for positive coverage, so you can rely on us to tell it like it is.

QuickStart Guide 7

Vienna Top Sights 8

Vienna Local Life 12

Vienna Day Planner 14

Need to Know 16

Vienna Neighbourhoods 18

Explore Vienna 21

22 Hofburg & Around

38 Historic Centre

54 Museum District

76 Karlsplatz

92 Schloss Belvedere to the Canal

Worth a Trip:

Prater 112

Schloss Schönbrunn 116

The Best of Vienna 123

Vienna's Best Walks

Essential Vienna **124**

Living History **126**

Vienna's Best...

Coffee Houses **128**

Food **130**

Drinking & Nightlife **132**

Entertainment **134**

Architecture **136**

Guided Tours **137**

Activities **138**

For Free **139**

For Kids **140**

Art **141**

Shopping **142**

Survival Guide 143

Before You Go **144**

Arriving in Vienna **145**

Getting Around **147**

Essential Information **148**

Language **152**

QuickStart Guide

Welcome to Vienna

With its imperial palaces, baroque streetscapes, chandelier-lit *Kaffeehäuser* (coffee houses) and wood-panelled *Beisln* (bistro pubs), Vienna is infused with history. Yet not only does it hold on to its traditions, it continues to incorporate them in everything from design, architecture and contemporary art to eco initiatives and culinary innovations. Vienna's past is alive in its present and, by extension, its future.

Rooftop view of Vienna
ADISA/GETTY IMAGES ©

Vienna
Top Sights

Hofburg (p24)

Home to the Habsburg Empire for six and a half centuries, this monumental complex now harbours magnificent museums and attractions including the Spanish Riding School and the Burgkapelle's Vienna Boys' Choir Sunday Mass.

Stephansdom (p40)

Gothic architecture reaches its peak in Vienna's glorious cathedral, which rises in the city's historic heart. Tour the interior, climb its south tower for radiating views or delve into its skull-and-bone-packed catacombs.

Kunsthistorisches Museum (p56)

A treasure trove of art amassed by the Habsburgs fills Vienna's artistic jewel, the neoclassical Kunsthistorisches Museum. Its pièce de résistance is its Picture Gallery, which is packed with priceless Old Master paintings.

MuseumsQuartier
(p62)

Former imperial stables have been transformed into Vienna's Museums-Quartier. It brings together museums showcasing a wide spectrum of art, innovative performing arts venues and public spaces including courtyards, cafes and bars.

Naturhistorisches Museum (p66)

Sitting opposite the Kunsthistorisches Museum in a matching neoclassical building, the Naturhistorisches Museum time travels through four billion years of fascinating natural history illustrated through meteorites, dinosaurs and prehistoric and zoological displays.

Staatsoper (p78)

A roll-call of composers, including Mozart, Beethoven and Mahler, lived and worked in Vienna, and this City of Music's premier opera house, the lavish neo-Renaissance Staatsoper, is the ultimate place to catch a performance.

Schloss Belvedere (p94)

A baroque masterpiece, Schloss Belvedere lives up to its name 'beautiful view' in its tiered gardens overlooking Vienna's skyline and in the dazzling palace itself, which shelters the world's largest Klimt collection.

Prater (p112)

Amid the rambling woodlands, meadows and chestnut-shaded avenues of central Vienna's largest park are the Würstelprater's whirling fairground attractions crowned by Vienna's iconic 1897-built Ferris wheel, the Riesenrad.

Schloss Schönbrunn (p116)

Painted a sunny 'Schönbrunn Yellow', the Habsburgs' 1441-room summer palace is a Unesco World Heritage-listed wonder with opulent baroque interiors and spectacular formal gardens.

Vienna Local Life

Insider tips to help you find the real city

With its fairytale palaces and horse-drawn *Fiaker* carriages, all of Vienna could be a film set. Behind the scenes you'll encounter Viennese locals at design ateliers, back-street boutiques, hidden venues, hip cafes, canal-side beaches and *Schanigärten* (pavement terraces).

An Evening Out on the Town (p44)

▶ Illuminated streetscapes
▶ Local specialities

Vienna's historic centre overflows by day with workers, shoppers and sightseers but come nightfall, the crowds abate and the area offers a slice of Viennese life, when locals stroll the sepia-lit streets, stopping for a glass of regional wine, hearty Austrian cuisine, and strudel in a classic *Kaffeehaus* (coffee house).

Neubau's Design Scene (p68)

▶ Vienna-designed fashion
▶ Handmade homewares

The red-hot Viennese design scene is making its mark in art, accessories, fashion, furniture and homewares, and Neubau, adjoining the Museum District, is ground zero for the city's creatives and artisans. Scores of work-shops and showrooms have set up here, along with a slew of vintage shops, bars and cafes.

Epicure Tour of the Freihausviertel (p80)

▶ Regional produce
▶ Artisan products

Vienna's most vibrant market, the heady Naschmarkt, isn't the only foodie game in this neigh-bourhood. Fanning out from the Naschmarkt, the streets and laneways are crammed with bakeries, patisseries, chocolatiers, purveyors of farm-fresh produce and producers of local delicacies. Linger over a coffee, cake or glass of *Sekt* (sparkling wine).

Green Escape (p100)

▶ Idyllic parks
▶ Canal-side strolling

Thanks to progressive planning laws, green spaces comprise over 50% of the city – one of the key reasons Vienna regularly tops interna-tional quality of living surveys. Some of the loveliest local parks and gardens, including the city's botanic gardens, are here, along with lush, grassy stretches along the canal.

Rathausplatz Christkindlmarkt (p74)

Naschmarkt (p91)

Other great places to experience the city like a local:

Demel (p33)

Dorotheum (p37)

Wald & Wiese (p50)

Wiener Rosenmanufaktur (p52)

Christmas Markets (p74)

Eis Greissler (p86)

Naschmarkt (p91)

Zentralfriedhof (p106)

Lingenhel (p109)

Schanigärten (p110)

Vienna
Day Planner

Day One

Start your day at Vienna's heart, the **Stephansdom** (p40). Be awed by the cathedral's cavernous interior, Gothic stone pulpit and baroque high altar. For a bird's-eye view of Vienna, climb the cathedral's south tower to the viewing platform. Or delve below ground into its ossuary, the **Katakomben** (catacombs; p41). Spend the rest of the morning strolling the atmospheric narrow streets around the cathedral.

After delicious deli food and a glass of wine at the cafe/ wine bar adjoining **Meinl's Restaurant** (p33), make your way along Graben and Kohlmarkt to the **Hofburg** (p24), where one of the ultimate pleasures is simply to wander through and soak up the grandeur of this Habsburg architectural masterpiece. Narrow it down to one or two of the museums here, such as the **Kaiserappartements** (p25).

Dine on adventurous international 'journey menus' at **Blue Mustard** (p32) then head into the cobblestoned Spittelberg district to enduring favourites such as old-school brewery **Siebensternbräu** (p75) and hip new bars like the **Brickmakers Pub & Kitchen** (p74) for craft beers and ciders or **Le Troquet** (p75) for cocktails.

Day Two

Enjoy one of the city's best breakfasts at **Figar** (p73) before making your way to the **Kunsthistorisches Museum** (p56), where you can plan on spending at least a whole morning in the thrall of its Old Masters.

For lunch, duck behind the **MuseumsQuartier** (p62) to hidden **Glacis Beisl** (p74) for fortifying classics such as schnitzels. The afternoon is a good time to change artistic direction and explore at least one of the museums in the MuseumsQuartier. The light, bright **Leopold Museum** (p63) has splendid Austrian art. **MUMOK** (p63) makes a complete contrast, with contemporary, often controversial works. The MuseumsQuartier has plenty of bars if you need a break, such as the laid-back **Kantine** (p63).

Motto am Fluss (p50) has a hip lounge ambience on the Danube Canal. After dining, explore the Innere Stadt's streets and bar scene in the evening in the centre, sipping Austrian wines at **Vinothek W-Einkehr** (p44) and hitting architectural treasures such as **Zwölf Apostelkeller** (p52).

Short on time?

We've arranged Vienna's must-sees into these day-by-day itineraries to make sure you see the very best of the city in the time you have available.

Day Three

☀ Divide your morning between **Schloss Belvedere's** (p94) magnificently landscaped French-style formal **gardens** (p97) and its galleries. The **Unteres Belvedere** (p98) (Lower Belvedere) has baroque state apartments and ceremonial rooms, and hosts some superb temporary exhibitions in its orangery, while a walk through **Oberes Belvedere** (p95) (Upper Belvedere) takes you through a who's who of Austrian art.

☀ Refuel on goulash at **Meierei im Stadtpark** (p106). Then visit two of the outstanding museums in this neighbourhood, the **Heeresgeschichtliches Museum** (p104), covering 400 years of Austro-European military history, and the **Museum für Angewandte Kunst** (p104) (MAK), showcasing applied arts and crafts.

🌙 Cross the canal to the **Prater** (p112), Vienna's playground of woods, meadows and sideshow attractions at the **Würstelprater** (p113). The highlight here is the 19th-century **Riesenrad** (p113) Ferris wheel, famed for its role in 1949 film *The Third Man*, the James Bond instalment *The Living Daylights* and art-house favourite *Before Sunrise*.

Day Four

☀ Take an eye-popping tour of baroque extravaganza **Schloss Schönbrunn** (p116) and stroll the French formal **gardens** (p118), detouring to the **Gloriette** (p118), with breathtaking views of the palace and city skyline beyond.

☀ Browse the **Naschmarkt** (p91) for picnic supplies or stop at one of its sit-down eateries. Then continue to another baroque jewel, the **Karlskirche** (p84), and ride the lift (elevator) into the dome for an up-close view of its stunning fresco by Johann Michael Rottmayr. Take a break at one of the many cafe terraces overlooking the market. Then head to **Secession** (p84) to see seminal works by members of the Vienna Secession including Klimt's 34m-long *Beethoven Frieze*.

🌙 Neo-*Beisl* **Silberwirt** (p86) is a brilliant spot for innovatively prepared local and/or organic produce. The Margareten (the 5th district) and Mariahilf (the 6th), both flanking the trickling Wien River, offer plenty of drinking and nightlife opportunities. Sip *Sekt* (sparkling wine) at **Sekt Comptoir** (p81), enjoy a pint at **Café Rüdigerhof** (p87), and hit the dance floor at **Club U** (p88).

Need to Know

For more information, see Survival Guide (p143)

Currency
Euro (€)

Language
German

Visas
Generally not required for stays of up to 90 days (or at all for EU nationals); some nationalities need a Schengen visa.

Money
ATMs are widely available. Credit cards are not always accepted in budget hotels or budget to midrange restaurants. Bars and cafes usually only accept cash.

Mobile Phones
Check with your service provider about using your phone in Austria and roaming costs, especially for data.

Time
Central European Time (GMT/UTC plus one hour)

Tipping
Restaurants and cafes Tips are generally expected; round up smaller bills (to the nearest 50 cents or euro) when buying coffee or beer, and add 5% to 10% to the bill for full meals. Tip at the time of payment as one lump sum with the bill.

Taxis Drivers will expect around 10% extra.

Hotel porters and cloakroom attendants Tip a euro or two.

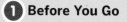 **Before You Go**

Your Daily Budget

Budget: Less than €100
► Dorm bed: €25–30
► Cheap double per person: €40–65
► Self-catering or lunchtime specials: €6–12
► Free sights and cheap museums: up to €7

Midrange: €100–180
► Hotel double per person: €65–105
► Two-course midrange meal with glass of wine: €25–35
► High profile museums: €13

Top end: Over €180
► Upmarket hotel double per person: from €105
► Multicourse meal with wine: from €70
► Opera and theatre: from €40

Useful Websites

Tourist Info Wien (www.wien.info) Vienna's tourist office.

Lonely Planet (www.lonelyplanet.com/vienna) Destination information, hotel bookings, traveller forum and more.

Vienna Webservice (www.wien.gv.at) City council website.

Advance Planning

Three months before Reserve tickets for major performances and events.

One month before Make reservations for top-shelf restaurants.

One week before Check Falter (www.falter.at) for a table in popular restaurants for weekend nights.

② Arriving in Vienna

✈ From Vienna International Airport

The City Airport Train (CAT; €11, 15 minutes) leaves the airport every 30 minutes from 6.09am till 11.39pm 365 days. The cheaper but slower S7 suburban train (€4.40, 25 minutes) also runs every 30 minutes from 4.48am to 12.18am from the airport to Wien-Mitte. Expect to pay €25 to €50 for a taxi.

🚊 From Wien Hauptbahnhof

Situated 3km south of Stephansdom, Vienna's gleaming-new main train station handles all international trains as well as trains from all of Austria's provincial capitals, and many local and regional trains. It's linked to the centre by U-Bahn line 1, trams D and O, and buses 13A and 69A. A taxi to the centre costs about €10. All stations are generally safe late at night and have good connections with the centre and suburbs.

③ Getting Around

U U-Bahn

Fast, comfortable and safe. Trains run from 5am to midnight Monday to Thursday and continuously from 5am Friday through to midnight Sunday. Tickets are sold at machines or windows at stations. Validate tickets prior to boarding.

🚋 Tram

Slower but more enjoyable. Depending on route, trams run from around 5.15am to about 11.45pm. Buy tickets at kiosks or from the driver (more expensive). Validate tickets when boarding.

🚌 Bus

Reliable, punctual, with several very useful routes for visitors. Most run from 5am to midnight; services can be sporadic or non-existent on weekends. Tickets can be bought from the driver or from a *Tabakladen* (tobacconist). Validate tickets on boarding.

🚌 Night Bus

Especially useful for outer areas; runs every 30 minutes from 12.30am to 5am. Main stops are located at Schwedenplatz, Schottentor and Kärntner Ring/Oper.

ᚖ Bicycle

Over 120 Citybike Wien bike-share stands are located across the city.

Vienna
Neighbourhoods

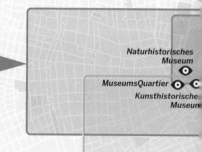

Hofburg & Around (p22)
The rambling Hofburg complex is the centrepiece of this neighbourhood.

⊙ Top Sight
Hofburg

Museum District (p54)
Art is everywhere in this neighbourhood's masterpiece-packed museums.

⊙ Top Sights
Kunsthistorisches Museum

MuseumsQuartier

Naturhistorisches Museum

Naturhistorisches Museum ⊙

MuseumsQuartier ⊙ ⊙

Kunsthistorisches Museum

⊙
Schloss Schönbrunn

Karlsplatz (p76)
Home to tantalising markets, artisan shops, lively nightlife venues and outstanding entertainment.

⊙ Top Sights
Staatsoper

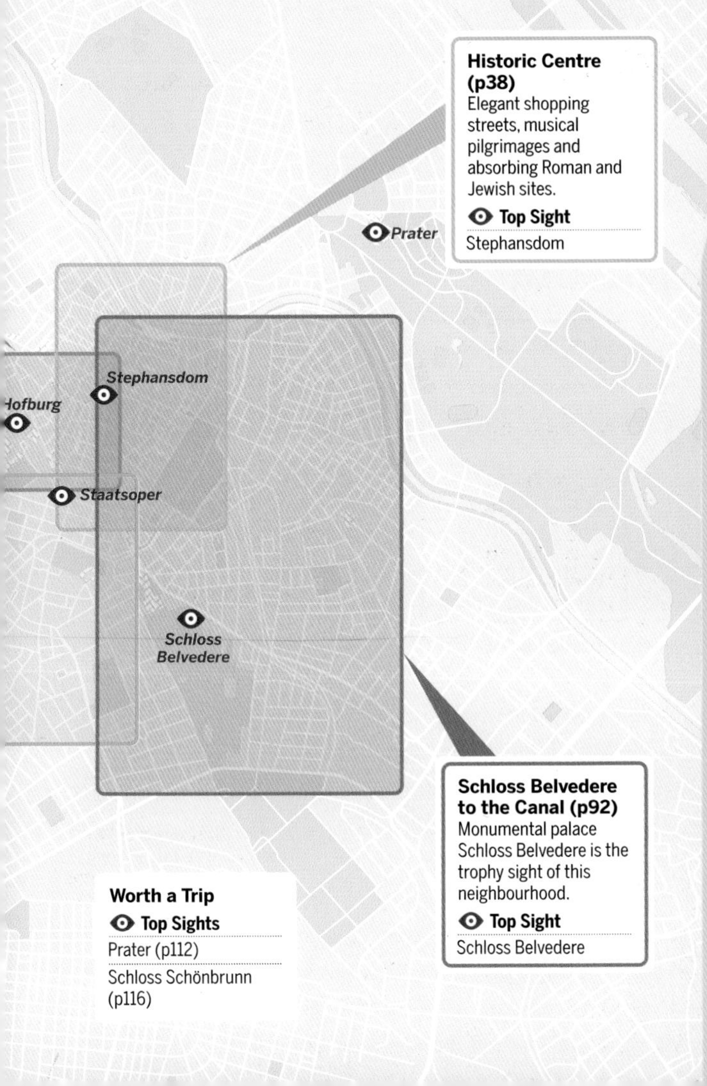

Historic Centre (p38)
Elegant shopping streets, musical pilgrimages and absorbing Roman and Jewish sites.

◉ **Top Sight**
Stephansdom

◉ Prater

◉ Hofburg

◉ Stephansdom

◉ Staatsoper

◉ Schloss Belvedere

Schloss Belvedere to the Canal (p92)
Monumental palace Schloss Belvedere is the trophy sight of this neighbourhood.

◉ **Top Sight**
Schloss Belvedere

Worth a Trip
◉ **Top Sights**
Prater (p112)
Schloss Schönbrunn (p116)

Explore
Vienna

Hofburg & Around **22**

Historic Centre **38**

Museum District **54**

Karlsplatz **76**

Schloss Belvedere to the Canal .. **92**

Worth a Trip

Prater 112
Schloss Schönbrunn 116

Tourists wander along Graben (p53)
SHCHIPKOVA ELENA/SHUTTERSTOCK ©

Explore

Hofburg & Around

Vienna's imperial splendour peaks in this part of the Innere Stadt (city centre), where *Fiaker* (horse-drawn carriages) prance along curved, cobbled streets. Its centrepiece is the magnificent Hofburg palace complex, which brims with museums and world-famous attractions including the waltzing horses of the Spanish Riding School. Museums also abound in the streets north towards Stephansplatz.

The Sights in a Day

The monumental **Hofburg** (p24) was the seat of the Habsburgs for some six and a half centuries and is one of the most spectacular palace complexes in the Austrian capital. The grandest place to start is at the gate on Michaelerplatz, where the Habsburgs used to enter. From here you can stroll from one end to the other in about an hour, with time to stop and admire the architecture. If you plan on visiting several Hofburg museums, block your calendar for much of the day to see these comfortably.

Exquisite sandwiches from **Trześniewski** (p33) are perfect for lunch on the run. Plan to spend at least another four hours taking in the most important sights around the Hofburg – the **Albertina** (p30) graphic-arts gallery, **Kaisergruft** (p30), where most of the Habsburg royal family are buried, and the **Jüdisches Museum** (Jewish Museum; p48). There's great shopping here too.

After dinner at stunning new restaurant/cocktail bar **Blue Mustard** (p32), drop by an iconic Viennese coffee house like **Café Leopold Hawelka** (p34) and/or a classic bar such as **Loos American Bar** (p34).

👁 Top Sights

Hofburg (p24)

💜 Best of Vienna

Coffee Houses

Café Leopold Hawelka (p34)

Demel (p33)

Food

Blue Mustard (p32)

Bitzinger Würstelstand am Albertinaplatz (p25)

Trześniewski (p33)

Entertainment

Burgkapelle (p26)

Hofburg Concert Halls (p35)

Shopping

Steiff (p37)

Dorotheum (p37)

Getting There

Ⓤ **U-Bahn** Herrengasse (U3) and Stephansplatz (U1, U3) are closest to the Hofburg.

🚊 **Tram** Useful for entering from Ringstrasse (D, 1, 2, 71 Dr-Karl-Renner-Ring, Burgring and Kärntner Ring/Oper).

Top Sights
Hofburg

Built as a fortified castle in the 13th century, the home of the Habsburg rulers from Rudolph I in 1279 until the Austrian monarchy collapsed under Karl I in 1918 is the ultimate display of Austria's former imperial power. Today, the impressive palace complex contains the offices of the Austrian president, an ensemble of extraordinary museums and stately public squares.

 Map p28, D3

Imperial Palace

www.hofburg-wien.at

01, Michaelerkuppel

general admission free

🚌 1A, 2A Michaelerplatz,
🚋 D, 1, 2, 46, 49, 71 Burgring,
Ⓤ Herrengasse

Kaiserappartements

The **Kaiserappartements** (Imperial Apartments; adult/child €12.90/7.70, incl guided tour €15.90/9.20; ⊙9am-6pm Jul & Aug, to 5.30pm Sep-Jun) were once the official living quarters of Franz Josef I (1830–1916) and Empress Elisabeth (1837–98; or Sisi, as she was affectionately named). The highlight is the **Sisi Museum**, devoted to Austria's most beloved empress, which has a strong focus on the clothing and jewellery of Austria's monarch and a replica of her personal fitness room complete with rings and bars. Also here is a reconstruction of Sisi's luxurious Pullman coach. Many of the empress's famous portraits are also on show, as is her death mask, made after her assassination in Geneva in 1898.

Multilingual audio guides are included in the admission price. Guided tours take in the Kaiserappartements, the Sisi Museum and the adjoining **Silberkammer**, whose largest silver service caters to 140 dinner guests.

Kaiserliche Schatzkammer

The **Kaiserliche Schatzkammer** (Imperial Treasury; www.kaiserliche-schatzkammer.at; 01, Schweizerhof; adult/child €12/free; ⊙9am-5.30pm Wed-Mon) contains secular and ecclesiastical treasures of priceless value and splendour – the sheer wealth of this collection of crown jewels is staggering. As you walk through the rooms you see a golden rose, diamond-studded Turkish sabres, a 2680-carat Colombian emerald and, the highlight of the treasury, the imperial crown. The wood-panelled **Sacred Treasury** has a collection of rare religious relics: fragments of the True Cross, the Holy Lance that pierced Jesus on the Cross, one of the nails from the Crucifixion, a thorn from Christ's crown and a piece of tablecloth from the Last Supper. Multilingual audio guides cost €4

☑ **Top Tips**

▶ If you plan on visiting several attractions in and around the Hofburg, various combination tickets not only save you money but will also save you time spent queuing for individual tickets.

▶ Book several months ahead for Spanish Riding School performances and at least a month ahead for standing-room tickets.

✕ **Take a Break**

Stop by for a classic Viennese sausage at **Bitzinger Würstelstand am Albertinaplatz** (www.bitzinger-wien.at; 01, Albertinaplatz; sausages €3.40-4.40; ⊙8am-4am; 🚊Kärntner Ring/Oper, Ⓤ Karlsplatz, Stephansplatz).

Take a seat on the terrace or in the art nouveau interior of the beautiful **Palmenhaus** (☏01-533 10 33; www. palmenhaus.at; 01, Burggarten; ⊙10am-midnight Mon-Fri, 9am-midnight Sat, 9am-11pm Sun; 🚊D, 1, 2, 71 Burgring, Ⓤ Karlsplatz, Museumsquartier) for a drink or a traditional Austrian meal.

(the shorter highlight audio tour is free) and are very worthwhile.

Burgkapelle

The **Burgkapelle** (Royal Chapel; ☎01-533 99 27; www.hofmusikkapelle.gv.at; 01, Schweizer Hof; ⊙10am-2pm Mon & Tue, 11am-1pm Fri; ⊟2A Heldenplatz, ⊟D, 1, 2, 71 Burgring, Ⓤ Herrengasse) originally dates from the 13th century. It received a Gothic makeover from 1447 to 1449, but much of this disappeared during the baroque fad. Its vaulted wooden statuary survived and is testament to those Gothic days. The **Vienna Boys' Choir Mass** (tickets €10-36) takes place here every Sunday at 9.15am between September and June. The chapel is sometimes closed to visitors in July and August, so check ahead in those months.

Spanish Riding School

The world-famous **Spanish Riding School** (Spanische Hofreitschule; ☎01-533 90 31-0; www.srs.at; 01, Michaelerplatz 1; performances €25-217; ⊙hours vary) is a Viennese institution truly reminiscent of the imperial Habsburg era. This unequalled equestrian show is performed by Lipizzaner stallions formerly kept at an imperial stud established at Lipizza (hence the name). These graceful stallions perform an equine ballet to a program of classical music while the audience watches from pillared balconies – or from a

Hofburg Palace

Volksgarten

Schauflergasse

Herren-gasse

Kohlmarkt

Habsburgergasse

Michaelerplatz

Kaiser-appartements 🄰

In der Burg

Reitschulgasse

Braunerstr

Spanish Riding School

Heldenplatz

Monument to Archduke Karl 🄱

Josefsplatz

Dorotheergasse

Kaiserliche Schatzkammer 🄲 Burgkapelle

Burgring (Ringstrasse)

Neue Burg Museums 🏛

Augustinerstr

Hanuschgasse

Maria-Theresien-Platz

Burggarten

Helmut-Zilk-Platz (Albertinaplatz)

cheaper standing-room area – and the chandeliers shimmer above.

There are many different ways to see the Lipizzaner. **Performances** are the top-shelf variant, and for seats at these you will need to book several months in advance. The website lists performance dates and you can order tickets online. As a rule of thumb, performances are at 11am on Sunday from mid-February to June and mid-August to December, with frequent additional performances on Saturday and occasionally other days of the week. For standing-room tickets, book at least one month in advance. During the summer break, it hosts special 'Piber meets Vienna' performances. Visitors to the **Morgenarbeit** can drop in for part of a session (morning training sessions; adult/child €15/7.50, 10am to noon Tuesday to Friday January to June and mid-August to December).

One-hour **guided tours** (adult/child €16/8; 2pm, 3pm and 4pm March to late January, 2pm 3pm and 4pm Tuesday to Sunday late January and February), held in English and German, take you into the performance hall, stables and other facilities. A combined **morning training and tour** (adult/child €31/15) is another option. The visitor centre here sells all tickets.

Neue Burg Museums

The **Neue Burg Museums** (☏ 01-525 240; www.khm.at; 01, Heldenplatz; adult/child €15/free; ☉ 10am-6pm Wed-Sun; 🚆 D,

Empress Elisabeth (Sisi)

Empress Maria Theresia (1717–80) is immortalised in her robed, operatic glory in the middle of Maria-Theresien-Platz, but Empress Elisabeth, better know as Sisi, is the real darling of the Habsburg show in this part of town. The cult of Sisi knows no bounds in German-speaking countries, due in large part to the trilogy of films from the 1950s starring Austro-French actress Romy Schneider. Schneider embodied the empress so well that in the popular mind it often seems hard to distinguish Sisi as art and the empress in reality.

1, 2, 71 Burgring, Ⓤ Herrengasse, Museumsquartier) comprise the **Sammlung alter Musikinstrumente** (Collection of Ancient Musical Instruments), with a diverse array of instruments; the **Ephesos Museum** featuring artefacts unearthed during Austrian archaeologists' excavations at Ephesus, Turkey, between 1895 to 1906; and the **Hofjagd- und Rüstkammer** (Arms and Armour), containing ancient armour dating mainly from the 15th and 16th centuries. An audio guide costs €4.

For reviews see

- 👁 Top Sights — p24
- ◉ Sights — p30
- ✕ Eating — p32
- 🍷 Drinking — p34
- ⭐ Entertainment — p35
- 🔒 Shopping — p37

Am Hof
Irisgasse
Haarhof
9 ✕
🍷 15
Bognergasse
Naglergasse
Seitzergasse
Tuchlauben
Brandstätte
Milchgasse

ahnen-
gasse
Wallnerstr
Kohlmarkt
10 ✕
Jungferngasse
Graben
Goldschmiedgasse
Jasomirgottstr
Trattnerhof
Stephans-
platz

Michaeler-
platz
Reitschulestr
Habsburgergasse
Bräunerstr
🔒 17
11 🍷
7 ✕
✕ 8
Stock-im-
Eisen-Platz
Stephansplatz
Churhaus-
gasse
Singerstr

Dorotheergasse
Spiegelgasse
Plankengasse
Josefsplatz
Seilergasse
Kärntner
Durchgang
12
Neuer Markt
Kärntner Str
Weihburggasse
Lillengasse
Rauhensteingasse
Ballgasse

4 ◉ Nationalbibliothek
Prunksaal
2 ◉
Augustinerkirche ◉
Theater-
Museum
◉ 6
Augustinerstr
Gluckgasse
Lobkowitz-
platz
Kaisergruft
3 ◉
Marco-
d'Aviano-
Gasse
18 🔒
Himmelpfortgasse
Johannesgasse

Hanuschgasse
Albertina
1 ◉
Tegetthoffstr
🔒 19
ℹ Tourist Info Wien
Führichgasse
Maysedergasse
Kärntner Str
Annagasse
Seilerstätte

Goethegasse
Operngasse
Philharmonikerstr
Krugerstr
Fichte-
gasse

Sights

Albertina
GALLERY

1 ⊙ Map p28, F5

Once used as the Habsburgs' imperial apartments for guests, the Albertina is now a repository for what's regularly touted as the greatest collection of graphic art in the world. The permanent Batliner Collection – with over 100 paintings covering the period from Monet to Picasso – and the high quality of changing exhibitions really make the Albertina worthwhile.Multilingual audio guides (€4) cover all of the exhibition sections and tell the story behind the apartments and the works on display. (www.albertina.at; 01, Albertinaplatz 3; adult/child €12.90/free; ⊙10am-6pm Thu-Tue, to 9pm Wed; ⛴D, 1, 2, 71 Kärntner Ring/Oper, Ⓤ Karlsplatz, Stephansplatz)

Augustinerkirche
CHURCH

2 ⊙ Map p28, E4

The real highlight of the 14th-century Gothic Augustinerkirche (Augustinian Church) is not its pale, vaulted interior but a crypt containing silver urns with the hearts of 54 Habsburg rulers. The church hosts regular evening classical music concerts. See the website (http://hochamt. augustiner.at) for further details. Sometimes on a visit you can catch the choir practising. The crypt is open on Sunday after the 11am Mass (celebrated with a full choir and orchestra) – turn up around 12.30pm. Many Habsburg weddings took place here. (📞01-533 09 470; http://augustinerkirche.augustiner.at; 01, Augustinerstrasse 3; admission free; ⊙8am-6pm, hours can vary; ⛴1A, 2A Michaelerplatz, Ⓤ Herrengasse)

Kaisergruft
MAUSOLEUM

3 ⊙ Map p28, F4

Beneath the **Kapuzinerkirche** (Church of the Capuchin Friars; www.erzdioezese-wien.at; ⊙8am-6pm), the Kaisergruft is the final resting place of most of the Habsburg royal family, including beloved Empress Elisabeth. Opened in 1633, it was instigated by Empress Anna (1585–1618). Her body and that of her husband, Emperor Matthias (1557–1619), were the first entombed in this impressive vault. A total of 149 Habsburgs are buried here, including 12 emperors and 19 empresses. English-language, 30-minute guided tours (included in admission) take place at 3.30pm Wednesday to Saturday. (Imperial Burial Vault; www.kaisergruft.at; 01, Tegetthoffstrasse 2; adult/child €5.50/2.50; ⊙10am-6pm; ⛴D, 1, 2, 71 Kärntner Ring/Oper, Ⓤ Stephansplatz, Karlsplatz)

Nationalbibliothek Prunksaal
LIBRARY

4 ⊙ Map p28, E4

Austria's flagship library, the Nationalbibliothek, contains an astounding collection of literature, maps, globes of the world and other cultural

Albertina

relics; its highlight, though, is the **Prunksaal** (Grand Hall), a majestic baroque hall built between 1723 and 1726, with a fresco by Daniel Gran. Commissioned by Karl VI (whose statue is under the central dome), the library holds some 200,000 leather-bound scholarly tomes. Audio guides cost €3. (📞 01-534 10; www.onb. ac.at; 01, Josefsplatz 1; adult/child €7/free; ⏰ 10am-6pm Tue, Wed & Fri-Sun, to 9pm Thu; 🚊 D, 1, 2, 71 Burgring, Ⓤ Herrengasse)

Globenmuseum   MUSEUM

5 ◉ Map p28, D2

Part of the Nationalbibliothek collection of museums, along with the **Esperantomuseum** (located on the ground floor) and **Papyrusmuseum** (📞 01-534 10 420; 01, Heldenplatz; ⏰ 10am-6pm Tue, Wed & Fri-Sun, to 9pm Thu; 🚊 D, 1, 2, 71 Burgring, Ⓤ Herrengasse, Museumsquartier) – admission covers all three; audio guides are available for €2 – this small museum, which is situated inside a former palace (Palais Mollard), is completely dedicated to cartography. Among the impressive collection of 19th-century globes and maps are some true gems dating from the 16th century. Make sure to look out for the globe made for Emperor Karl V by Mercator in 1541. (📞 01-534 10 710; www. onb.ac.at; 01, Herrengasse 9, 1st fl; adult/ child €4/free; ⏰ 10am-6pm Fri-Wed, to 9pm Thu Jun-Sep 10am-6pm Tue, Wed & Fri-Sun, to

9pm Thu Oct-May; 🚎1A, 2A Michaelerplatz,
Ⓤ Herrengasse)

TheaterMuseum   MUSEUM

6 ◉ Map p28, F4

Housed in the baroque Lobkowitz
palace (1694), this museum has a
permanent exhibition devoted to

Top Tip

Combination Tickets

Combined options for the Hofburg
and nearby museums include the
following:

▶ **Sisi Ticket** (adult/child
€28.80/17) Includes the Imperial Apartments, Sisi Museum and
Silberkammer (Imperial Silver
Collection) with audio guide, as
well as Schloss Schönbrunn and
the Hofmobiliendepot (Imperial
Furniture Collection).

▶ **Schatz der Habsburger**
(Treasures of the Habsburgs; adult/
child €20/free) Includes Kunsthistorisches Museum, Neue Burg and
Kaiserliche Schatzkammer.

▶ **Masterticket** (adult/child €24/
free) Includes the Neue Burg Museums, Kunsthistorisches Museum
and the Leopold Museum.

▶ **Die Kostbarkeiten des Kaisers**
(Treasures of the Emperors; adult/
child €23/free) Includes the Kaiserliche Schatzkammer and Morgenarbeit (morning training sessions) at
the Spanish Riding School.

Austrian composer Gustav Mahler
(1860–1911) and temporary exhibitions dedicated to Vienna's theatre
history. Since 2014, it has also
displayed the collection from the
Staatsoper's former museum with
portraits of operatic greats, costumes, stage designs and documents
spotlighting premieres and highlights like Karajan's eight-year reign
as director. Opera lovers will enjoy
the occasional gem, such as Dame
Margot Fonteyn's stub-toed ballet
slipper. (📞01-525 24 3460; www.theater-
museum.at; 01, Lobkowitzplatz 2; adult/child
incl all exhibitions €8/free; ⊙10am-6pm
Wed-Mon; 🚋D, 1, 2, 62, 71 Kärntner Ring/
Oper, Ⓤ Stephansplatz)

Eating

Blue Mustard   INTERNATIONAL €€

7 🍽 Map p28, F3

Backlit wood hand-carvings of
Stephansdom's Gothic windows, a
wall-to-wall neon-lit map of Vienna
and a street-food truck parked in the
foyer make this one of Vienna's hottest new openings. Alexander Mayer's
'Journey menus' might start in Vienna
(*Beuschel* veal ragout) and end in
Naples (*Torta Ricotta e Pera* – poached
pear and ricotta in an almond-and-
hazelnut biscotti) with spectacular
cocktail pairings. (📞01-934 67 05; www.
bluemustard.at; 01, Dorotheergasse 6-8;
4-course menus €59-63, mains €15-25,
street food €4.50-8.50; ⊙kitchen 5-10pm
Mon-Sat, street-food truck 8am-5pm Mon-Sat,

bar 5pm-2am Mon-Thu, 5pm-4am Fri & Sat;
U Stephansplatz)

Trześniewski   SANDWICHES €

8 🍴 Map p28, G2

Trześniewski has been serving
exquisite open-faced finger-style
sandwiches for over 100 years. Choose
from 22 delectable toppings incor-
porating primarily Austrian-sourced
produce – chicken liver, smoked
salmon and horseradish cream cheese
and wild paprika and red pepper, egg
and cucumber – on dark Viennese
bread. This branch is the flagship
of a now 10-strong chain in Vienna.
(www.trzesniewski.at; 01, Dorotheergasse 1;
sandwiches €1.20-3.60; ⏱8.30am-7.30pm
Mon-Fri, 9am-6pm Sat, 10am-5pm Sun;
U Stephansplatz)

Bierhof   AUSTRIAN €€

9 🍴 Map p28, E1

A narrow passageway opens to a
courtyard where umbrella-shaded
tables beneath the trees make a
charming spot to dine on homemade
classics like *Eiernockerl* (flour-
and-egg dumplings), *Tiroler Gröstl*
(pork, potatoes and bacon, topped
with a fried egg), *Tiroler Leber* (liver
dumplings with apple sauce and
green beans) and *Wiener Schnitzel*
with parsley potatoes. The mid-week
lunch menu costs just €7.10. (📞01-533
44 28; http://bierhof.at; 01, Haarhof 3; mains
€9.90-23.90; ⏱11.30am-11.30pm; 📶;
U Herrengasse)

Local Life
The Sacher Torte

Eduard Sacher, the son of the
Sacher Torte creator Franz
Sacher, began working at **Demel**
(Map p28, E2; www.demel.at; 01,
Kohlmarkt 14; ⏱9am-7pm; 🚌1A,
2A Michaelerplatz, U Herrengasse,
Stephansplatz) in 1934, bringing the
original recipe and sole distribu-
tion rights with him. Between
1938 and 1963 legal battles raged
between Demel and Café Sacher
over the trademark and title. An
out-of-court settlement gave **Café
Sacher** (Map p28, F5; www.sacher.
com; 01, Philharmonikerstrasse 4;
⏱8am-midnight; 🚋D, 1, 2, 71 Kärntner
Ring/Oper, U Karlsplatz) the rights to
the phrase 'Original Sacher Torte',
and Demel the rights to decorate
with a seal reading 'Eduard-
Sacher-Torte'. Both cafes claim to
be a cut above the other; try both
and decide.

Meinl's
Restaurant   INTERNATIONAL €€€

10 🍴 Map p28, F1

Meinl's combines cuisine of superla-
tive quality with an unrivalled wine
list and views of Graben. Creations
at its high-end restaurant span
calamari and white-truffle risotto,
apple schnapps-marinated pork fillet
with green beans and chanterelles.
Its on-site **providore** (⏱8am-7.30pm
Mon-Fri, 9am-6pm Sat) has a cafe and

sushi bar, and its cellar **wine bar** (🕐11am-midnight Mon-Sat) serves great-value lunch menus. (📞01-532 33 34 6000; www.meinlamgraben.at; 01, Graben 19; mains €16-39, 4-/5-course menus €67/85; 🕐noon-midnight Mon-Sat; 🛜📶; Ⓤ Stephansplatz)

Drinking

Café Leopold Hawelka
COFFEE

11 🚇 Map p28, F3

Opened in 1939 by Leopold and Josefine Hawelka, whose son Günter still bakes the house-speciality *Buchteln* (sweet jam-filled, sugar-dusted yeast rolls) to Josefine's secret recipe today, this low-lit, picture-plastered coffee house is truly a living slice of Viennese history. It was once the hangout of artists and writers – Friedensreich Hundertwasser, Elias Canetti, Arthur Miller and Andy Warhol included. (www.hawelka.at; 01, Dorotheergasse 6; 🕐8am-midnight Mon-Wed, to 1am Thu-Sat, 10am-midnight Sun; Ⓤ Stephansplatz)

Loos American Bar
COCKTAIL BAR

12 🚇 Map p28, G3

Loos is *the* spot in the Innere Stadt for a classic cocktail such as its signature dry martini, expertly whipped up by talented mixologists. Designed by Adolf Loos in 1908, this tiny 27 sq metre box (seating just 20-or-so patrons) is bedecked from head to toe in onyx and polished brass, with mirrored walls that make it appear far larger. (www.loosbar.at; 01, Kärntner Durchgang 10; 🕐noon-5am Thu-Sat, to 4am Sun-Wed; Ⓤ Stephansplatz)

Café Central
CAFE

13 🚇 Map p28, D1

Coffee house legend alert: Trotsky came here to play chess, and turn-of-the-century literary greats like Karl Kraus and Peter Bahr regularly met here for coffee. Its marble pillars, arched ceilings and chandeliers now mostly play host to tourists, and the queues can be tedious, but once in it's a deliciously storied setting for a *melange* and slices of chocolate-truffle *Altenbergtorte*. (www.palaisevents.at; 01, Herrengasse 14; 🕐7.30am-10pm Mon-Sat, 10am-10pm Sun; 🛜; Ⓤ Herrengasse)

Volksgarten ClubDiskothek
CLUB

14 🚇 Map p28, B3

Spilling onto the Volksgarten's lawns, these early 19th-century premises are split into three areas: the Wintergarten lounge bar with vintage 1950s furnishings and palms, Cortic Säulenhalle ('column hall'), hosting live music and theme nights, and hugely popular ClubDiskothek (cover charge from €3). Hours vary; check the program online. (http://volksgarten.at; 01, Burgring 1; 🕐Apr–mid-Sep; 🚊D, 1, 2, 71 Dr-Karl-Renner-Ring, Ⓤ Museumsquartier, Volkstheater)

Original Sacher Torte at Café Sacher (p33)

Esterházykeller

WINE BAR

15 Map p28, E1

Tucked in a quiet courtyard just off Kohlmarkt, this *Heurigen* (wine tavern) has an enormous cellar – rustic decor, complete with medieval weaponry and farming tools – where excellent wine is served direct from the Esterházy Palace wine estate in Eisenstadt, as well as beer. The adjoining Esterházy Stüberl (restaurant; mains €9.90 to €24.90) opens from 11am to 10pm September to June. (01-533 34 82; www.esterhazykeller.at; 01, Haarhof 1; 4-11pm Sep-Jun; Stephansplatz, Herrengasse)

Entertainment

Hofburg Concert Halls

CLASSICAL MUSIC

16 Map p28, D4

The Neue Hofburg's concert halls, the sumptuous Festsaal and Redoutensaal, are regularly used for Strauss and Mozart concerts, featuring the Hofburg Orchestra and soloists from the Staatsoper and Volksoper. Performances start at 8.30pm and tickets are available online and from travel agents and hotels. Seating is not allocated, so get in early. (01-587 25 52; www.hofburgorchester.at; 01, Heldenplatz; tickets €42-55; D, 1, 2, 71 Burgring, Herrengasse)

Understand
Composers at a Glance

Just some of the composers who hailed from Vienna or lived and worked in this musical city include the following:

Christoph Willibald Gluck (1714–87) Major works include *Orfeo* (1762) and *Alceste* (1767).

Wolfgang Amadeus Mozart (1756–91) Wrote some 626 pieces; among the greatest are *The Marriage of Figaro* (1786), *Don Giovanni* (1787) and *The Magic Flute* (1791). The Requiem Mass, written for his own death, remains one of the most powerful works in the classical canon.

Joseph Haydn (1732–1809) Wrote 108 symphonies, 68 string quartets, 47 piano sonatas and about 20 operas. His greatest works include Symphony No 102 in B-flat Major and the oratorios *The Creation* (1798).

Ludwig van Beethoven (1770–1827) Studied briefly with Mozart in Vienna in 1787; he returned in late 1792. At age 32, when he became almost totally deaf, ironically, Beethoven began writing some of his best works.

Franz Schubert (1797–1828) Raised in Vienna, Schubert was a prolific composer whose best-known works are his last symphony (the Great C Major Symphony), his Mass in E-flat and the Unfinished Symphony.

The Strausses & the Waltz The early masters of the genre were Johann Strauss the Elder (1804–49) and Josef Lanner (1801–43). Johann Strauss the Younger (1825–99) composed over 400 waltzes, including Vienna's unofficial anthem, *The Blue Danube* (1867).

Anton Bruckner (1824–96) Works include Symphony No 9, Symphony No 8 in C Minor and Mass in D Minor.

Johannes Brahms (1833–97) At the age of 29, Brahms moved to Vienna, where many of his works were performed by the Vienna Philharmonic. One of his best works is *Ein Deutsches Requiem*.

Gustav Mahler (1860–1911) Known mainly for his nine symphonies; best works include *Das Lied von der Erde* (The Song of the Earth) and Symphony Nos 1, 5 and 9.

Shopping

Steiff

TOYS

17 🔒 Map p28, F3

Founded in the late 19th century, Steiff is the original creator of the teddy bear, which it presented at the Leipzig Toy Fair in 1903: an American businessman bought 3000 and sold them under the name 'teddy bear' after US president Theodore ('Teddy') Roosevelt. Today its flagship shop is filled with adorable bears, along with other premium quality cuddly toys. (www.steiff-galerie-wien.at; 01, Bräunerstrasse 3; ⊙10am-12.30pm & 1.30-6pm Mon-Fri, 10am-12.30 & 1.30-5pm Sat; ⓊStephansplatz)

J&L Lobmeyr Vienna

HOMEWARES

18 🔒 Map p28, G4

Reached by a beautifully ornate wrought-iron staircase, this is one of Vienna's most lavish retail experiences. The collection of Biedermeier pieces, Loos-designed sets, fine/arty glassware and porcelain on display here glitters from the lights of the chandelier-festooned atrium. Lobmeyr has been in business since 1823, when it exclusively supplied the imperial court. (www.lobmeyr.at; 01, Kärntner Strasse 26; ⊙10am-7pm Mon-Fri, to 6pm Sat; Ⓤ Stephansplatz)

Local Life

Auction House

The **Dorotheum** (Map p28, F3; www.dorotheum.com; 01, Dorotheergasse 17; ⊙10am-6pm Mon-Fri, 9am-5pm Sat; ⓊStephansplatz) is among the largest auction houses in Europe and for the casual visitor it's more like a museum, housing everything from antique toys and tableware to autographs, antique guns and, above all, lots of quality paintings. You can bid at the regular auctions held here, otherwise just drop by (it's free) and enjoy browsing.

Bonbons Anzinger

CHOCOLATE

19 🔒 Map p28, F5

A jewel box of a chocolate shop, with ceramic-tiled floors, mint-green cabinets, and a dazzling array of handmade truffles and pralines, Bonbons Anzinger has a tiny upstairs tearoom serving coffee, tea and hot chocolate, with a chocolate on the side. Its speciality is the *Mozartkugel*, a dark chocolate-covered ball filled with pistachio marzipan and nougat, along with gingerbread at Christmas. (www.bonbons-anzinger.at; 01, Tegetthoffstrasse 7; ⊙8am-6.30pm Mon-Fri, 9am-6pm Sat, noon-4pm Sun; 🚃D, 1, 2, 71 Kärnter Ring/Oper, ⓊKarlsplatz)

Explore

Historic Centre

Vienna's heart beats in the streets surrounding its most distinctive landmark, the towering Gothic cathedral Stephansdom. With a tangle of cobbled lanes and elegant thoroughfares graced with pastel-shaded baroque buildings, the oldest part of the city incorporates the medieval Jewish quarter in the northwest and the stretch down to the canal's southern bank.

The Sights in a Day

☀ Vienna's entire Innere Stadt is compact and easily walked – especially its core, the **Stephansdom** (p40) and historic centre neighbourhood. The city's monumental cathedral makes an ideal starting point; plan to spend half a day exploring it in its entirety, including scaling the south tower's 343 steps for sweeping views over the Innere Stadt's rooftops.

☼ Stop for lunch at neo-*Beisl* **Huth Gastwirtschaft** (p49) before heading to the **Haus der Musik** (p48) and **Mozarthaus Vienna** (p48) to discover the Austrian capital's incredible musical heritage. Other key sights here include the **Museum Judenplatz** (p48).

☾ After dinner at charming **Griechenbeisl** (p48), night time is ideal for a romantic stroll through the illuminated streets.

For a local's day in the Historic Centre, see p44.

👁 Top Sights

Stephansdom (p40)

○ Local Life

An Evening Out on the Town (p44)

♥ Best of Vienna

Coffee Houses

Diglas (p52)

Prückel (p45)

Food

Griechenbeisl (p48)

Plachutta (p45)

Figlmüller (p50)

Huth Gastwirtschaft (p49)

Architecture

Stephansdom (p40)

For Kids

Haus der Musik (p48)

Getting There

Ⓤ **U-Bahn** Stephansplatz (U1, U3) and Schwedenplatz (U1, U4) are the main stops.

🚋 **Tram** Schwedenplatz (1, 2) and Kärntner Ring/Oper (1, 2, D, 71) are the most convenient stops.

Top Sights
Stephansdom

Soaring above the surrounding cityscape, Vienna's immense, filagreed Gothic masterpiece Stephansdom (St Stephan's Cathedral) – or Steffl (Little Stephan) as it's locally (and ironically) dubbed – symbolises the city like no other building. Highlights include the cathedral's spectacular main nave with its Gothic stone pulpit and baroque high altar, its *Katakomben* (catacombs), two towers and the cathedral treasures.

👁 Map p46. B4

📞 tours 01-515 323 054

01, Stephansplatz

main nave adult & one child €6, additional child €1.50

🕐 public visits 9am-11.30am & 1-4.30pm Mon-Sat, 1-4.30pm Sun

Ⓤ Stephansplatz

History

A church has stood on this site since the 12th century, reminders of which today are the Romanesque Riesentor (Giant Gate) and Heidentürme (Towers of the Heathens) at the entrance and above it. In 1359, at the behest of Habsburg Duke Rudolf IV, Stephansdom began receiving its Gothic makeover and Rudolf earned himself the epithet of 'The Founder' by laying the first stone in the reconstruction.

Stephansdom: Inside & Out

From outside the cathedral, the first thing that will strike you is the glorious tiled roof, with its dazzling row of chevrons on one end and the Austrian eagle on the other.

Inside the cathedral, the magnificent Gothic stone pulpit takes pride of place, fashioned in 1515 by Anton Pilgrim (his likeness appears in the stonework). The pulpit railing is adorned with salamanders and toads, symbolising the battle of good against evil.

At the far end of the main nave, the baroque high altar shows the stoning of St Stephen. The chancel to its left has the winged Wiener Neustadt altarpiece, dating from 1447; the right chancel has the Renaissance red-marble tomb of Friedrich III. Under his guidance the city became a bishopric (and the church a cathedral) in 1469.

Stephansdom Katakomben

The area around the cathedral was originally a graveyard. But with plague and influenza epidemics striking Europe in the 1730s, Karl VI ordered the graveyard to be closed and henceforth Vienna buried its dead beneath Stephansdom in the **Katakomben** (Catacombs; ☎ 01-515 523 054; 30min tour adult/child €5.50/2; ⏲ tours 10-11.30am

☑ Top Tips

▶ Admission to the side aisle (on the left, facing the altar) is free if you only want to gain a quick impression of the cathedral.

▶ For worshippers only, the main nave is free to enter during Mass. Outside these times, the main nave is open to the public (adult/child €6/1.50) or by audio-guided tours and guided tours. Along with the main nave, the *Katakomben* and lift/elevator to the north tower are closed during Mass (held up to eight times daily).

✗ Take a Break

Tuck into huge schnitzels at Figlmüller (p50), a beloved Vienna *Beisl* (small tavern).

Sigmund Freud's former haunt, the coffee house Café Korb (p50) is renowned for its schnitzel, sausages and apple strudel.

& 1.30-4.30pm Mon-Sat, 1.30-4.30pm Sun). Today, they contain the remains of countless victims, which are kept in a mass grave and a bone house. Also on display are rows of urns containing the internal organs of the Habsburgs. One of the many privileges of being a Habsburg was to be dismembered and dispersed after death: their hearts are in the Augustinerkirche in the Hofburg and the rest of their bodies are in the Kaisergruft. Entrance is allowed only on a tour.

Cathedral South Tower

When the foundation stone for the **south tower** (Südturm; adult/child €4.50/2; ⊙9am-5.30pm) was laid in 1359, Rudolf IV is said to have used a trowel and spade made of silver. Two towers were originally envisaged, but the Südturm grew so high that little space remained for the second; in 1433 the tower reached its final height of 136.7m. Today you can ascend the 343 steps to a small platform for one of Vienna's most spectacular views over the rooftops of the Innere Stadt (you don't need a ticket for the main nave).

Cathedral Pummerin

Weighing 21 tonnes, the **Pummerin** (Boomer Bell; adult/child €5.50/2; ⊙9am-5.30pm) is Austria's largest bell and was installed in the 68.3m-high **north tower** in 1957. While the rest of the cathedral was rising up in its new Gothic format, work was interrupted on this tower due to a lack of cash and

the fading allure of Gothic architecture. It's accessible only by lift; you don't need a ticket for the main nave.

Dom- & Diözesanmuseum

The **Dom- & Diözesanmuseum** (Cathedral & Diocesan Museum of Vienna; www. dommuseum.at) is a treasure trove of religious art pieces spanning a period of more than 1000 years. Among the collection's extraordinary exhibits are the earliest European portrait – of Duke Rudolph IV (1360) – and two Syrian glass vessels (1280–1310), thought to be among the oldest glass bottles in the world. Check the website for updates on its reopening following extensive renovations.

Guided Tours & Music

Multilingual audio guide tour The most common option to take in the cathedral interior; audio guides costing €8 per adult (including one child under 14; €1.50 per additional child).

They're available from 8.30am to 11.30am and 1pm to 5.30pm Monday to Saturday, and from 1pm to 5.30pm Sunday.

All-inclusive tour All-inclusive tours are partly with an audio guide, partly with a tour guide (adult €17.90, including one child under 14; €3 per additional child; seniors and students pay €13.90). Tours take in the cathedral interior, *Katakomben*, south tower and the north tower. Children aren't allowed to do it alone.

The interior of Stephansdom

Guided tours in English & German

English-language tours explain the background of the cathedral and walk you through its main interior features. The 30-minute tours leave at 10.30am Monday to Saturday (adult/child €5.50/2). The same guided tours in German leave at 3pm daily.

Evening roof-walk tours in German

These 90-minute south tower tours (adult/child €10/4) depart at 7pm every Saturday from July to September and feature a brisk climb to the top of the south tower.

Special events & Mass The website www.dommusik-wien.at has a program of special concerts and events, but the 10.15am Mass on Sundays (9.30am during the school holidays around July and August) is something really special, as it's conducted with full choral accompaniment. Tickets are available online at www.kunstkultur.com.

Local Life
An Evening Out on the Town

Vienna's Innere Stadt (inner city) has a wealth to see by day, but an evening stroll through its sepia-toned streets, passing floodlit monuments like the Stephansdom, provides a much more local perspective. You'll drink local wines, dine on Viennese specialities and see films from the Austrian Film Archive; you can also join the Viennese for late-night ice cream.

❶ Pre-dinner Drink

There are just 15 seats inside wine bar **Vinothek W-Einkehr** (☎0676 40 82 854; www.w-einkehr.at; 01, Laurenzerberg 1; ⏱3-10pm Tue-Fri, 4-10pm Sat; Ⓤ Schwedenplatz) and another eight on the summer terrace, so the action often spills onto the pavement (you can also reserve a table). All of the wines here are Austrian, from prestigious wine-growing regions including Blaufränkischland and Neusiedler See in Burgenland.

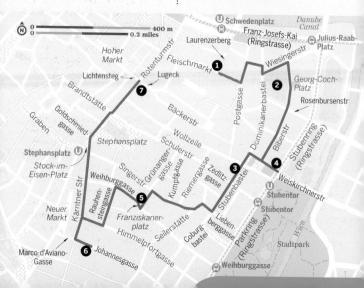

2 Jugendstil Design

Beautifully illuminated at night, the marble-cased and metal-'studded' **Postsparkasse** (Post Office Savings Bank; 01, Georg-Coch-Platz 2; museum adult/child 8/free; ⏰10am-5pm Mon-Fri; Ⓤ Schwedenplatz, 🚋1, 2) building is the Jugendstil work of Otto Wagner, who oversaw its construction between 1904 and 1906, and again from 1910 to 1912. It was innovative for its time, with a grey marble facade held together by 17,000 metal nails and an interior filled with sci-fi aluminium heating ducts and naked stanchions.

3 Dinner

If you're keen to taste Tafelspitz (boiled beef), you can't beat specialist white-tableclothed restaurant **Plachutta** (☎01-512 15 77; www.plachutta.at; 01, Wollzeile 38; mains €16.50-27.20; ⏰11.30am-11.15pm; Ⓤ Stubentor). It serves 13 varieties from different cuts of Austrian-reared beef, such as Mageres Meisel (lean, juicy shoulder meat), Beinfleisch (larded rib meat) and Lueger Topf (shoulder meat with beef tongue and calf's head). Save room for the Austrian cheese plate.

4 Dessert

Prückel (www.prueckel.at; 01, Stubenring 24; ⏰8.30am-10pm; 📶; 🚋2, Ⓤ Stubentor) features an intact 1950s design. Intimate booths, strong coffee, diet-destroying cakes and Prückel's speciality, its crispy, flaky apple strudel served with cream, are all big drawcards. Live piano music plays from 7pm to 10pm on Mondays, Wednesdays and Fridays.

5 Digestif

Designed by architect Hermann Czech in the 1970s, **Kleines Café** (01, Franziskanerplatz 3; ⏰10am-2am Mon-Sat, 1pm-2am Sun; 🚋2, Ⓤ Stubentor) has a bohemian atmosphere reminiscent of Vienna's heady Jugendstil days. It's tiny inside, but the wonderful summer outdoor seating on a cobbled square overlooking the baroque Franziskanerkirche is among the best in the Innere Stadt.

6 Movie Time

Part of the Austrian Film Archive, the **Metro Kinokulturhaus** (☎01-512 18 03; www.filmarchiv.at; 01, Johannesgasse 4; film tickets adult/child €8.50/7; ⏰2-9pm Mon-Fri, 11am-9pm Sat & Sun; Ⓤ Stephansplatz) opened in 2015 and is now its showcase for exhibitions (most free, some incurring an admission charge). The restored cinema here was first converted for screenings in 1924. It retains its wood panelling and red-velvet interior and shows historic and art-house Austrian films (in German).

7 Ice Cream

Opening to a vast summer terrace, Italian gelateria and pasticceria **Zanoni & Zanoni** (☎01-512 79 79; www.zanoni.co.at; 01, Lugeck 7; ice cream from €1.30; ⏰7.30am-midnight; Ⓤ Stephansplatz) has 30 seasonal varieties of gelato such as vanilla poppyseed, blueberry ricotta, strawberry and lemon, biscotto, tiramisu and chocolate and apricot. It also has vegan ice creams, frozen yoghurts and diabetic-friendly dishes including crêpes.

200 m
0.1 miles

Aspernbrückengasse

Zirkusgasse

Grosse Mohrengasse

Ferdinandstr

Praterstr

Aspernbrücke

Untere Donaustr

Julius-Raab-Platz

Julius-Raab-Platz

Wiesingstr

Georg-Coch-Platz

Biberstr

Rosenbursenstr

Schwedenbrücke

Taborstr

Greiselstr

Lilienbrunngasse

Hammer-Purgstall-Gasse

Friedrich-Wilhelm-Raiffeisen-Platz

Obere Donaustr

Marienbrücke

Postgasse

Dominikanerbastei

Postgasse

Laurenzerberg

9

Salztor-brücke

Danube Canal

Franz-Josefs-Kai (Ringstrasse)

Schwedenplatz

11 **10**

Rotenturmstr

Fleischmarkt

4

Grashof-gasse

Köllnerhofgasse

17

13

Schönlaterngasse

Jesuiten-gasse

Sonnenfelsgasse

Bäckerstr

Essig-gasse

Hollandstr

Salztorbrücke

15

Franz-Josefs-Kai

Morzin-platz

Rabensteig

Ruprechts-Stiege

14

Rabensteig

Marc-Aurel-Str

Salztorgasse

Gonzaga-gasse

Rudolfsplatz

Heinrichsgasse

Werdertorgasse

Gonzaga-gasse

Seitenstettengasse

Judengasse

Sterngasse

Vorlaufstr

Gölsdorfgasse

Hoher Markt

Salvatorgasse

Wipplingerstr

Lichtensteg

Rotenturmstr

Kramergasse

Bauernmarkt

Landskrongasse

Wildpret-markt

Brandstätte

Wolfzeile

Stephansdom

Jasomirgottstr

16

Goldschmiedgasse

Stephans-platz

Museum Judenplatz

Judenplatz

3

Parisergasse

Drahtgasse

Kurrentgasse

Tuchlauben

7

Milch-gasse

Peters-platz

Jungfern-gasse

Graben

Salzgries

Passauer Platz

Neutorgasse

Kärntner Durchgang

Kärntner Tor

A B C D E

1 2 3 4

47

For reviews see

◈ Top Sights   p40
◎ Sights   p48
✕ Eating   p48
◑ Drinking   p52
✷ Entertainment   p52
🛍 Shopping   p53

Sights

Haus der Musik
MUSEUM

1 ⊙ Map p46, B7

The Haus der Musik explains the world of sound and music to adults and children alike in an amusing and interactive way (in English and German). Exhibits are spread over four floors and cover everything from how sound is created, from Vienna's Philharmonic Orchestra to street noises. The staircase between floors acts as a piano; its glassed-in ground-floor courtyard hosts musical events. Admission is discounted after 8pm. The nearest tram stop is Kärntner Ring/Oper. (www.hausdermusik.com; 01, Seilerstätte 30; adult/child €13/6, with Mozarthaus Vienna €18/8; ⊙10am-10pm; 🚊D, 1, 2, 71; Ⓤ Karlsplatz)

Mozarthaus Vienna
MUSEUM

2 ⊙ Map p46, C5

The great composer spent 2½ happy and productive years at this residence between 1784 and 1787. Exhibits include copies of music scores and paintings, while free audio guides recreate the story of his time here. Mozart spent a total of 11 years in Vienna, changing residences frequently and sometimes setting up his home outside the Ringstrasse in the cheaper Vorstädte (inner suburbs) when his finances were tight. Of these the Mozarthaus Vienna is the only one that survives. (📞01-512 17 91; www.mozarthausvienna.at; 01, Domgasse 5; adult/child €11/4.50, with Haus der Musik €18/8; ⊙10am-7pm; Ⓤ Stephansplatz)

Museum Judenplatz
MUSEUM

3 ⊙ Map p46, A3

The main focus of Museum Judenplatz is on the excavated remains of a medieval synagogue that once stood on Judenplatz, with a film and numerous exhibits to elucidate Vienna's Jewish history. It was built in the Middle Ages, but Duke Albrecht V's 'hatred and misconception' led him to order its destruction in 1421. The basic outline of the synagogue can still be seen here. Combined tickets to the Museum Judenplatz and **Jüdisches Museum** (Jewish Museum; 01, Dorotheergasse 11; ⊙10am-6pm Sun-Fri) are valid for four days. (📞01-535 04 31; www.jmw.at; 01, Judenplatz 8; adult/child incl Jüdisches Museum €10/free; ⊙10am-6pm Sun-Thu, to 5pm Fri; Ⓤ Stephansplatz, Herrengasse)

Eating

Griechenbeisl
BISTRO €€

4 ✕ Map p46, C3

Dating from 1447 and frequented by Beethoven, Brahms, Schubert and Strauss among others, Vienna's oldest restaurant has vaulted rooms, wood panelling and a figure of Augustin trapped at the bottom of a well inside the front door. Every classic Viennese dish is on the menu, along with three daily vegetarian options. In summer, head to the plant-fringed front garden. (📞01-533 19 77; www.griechenbeisl.at; 01, Fleischmarkt 11; mains €15-28; ⊙11.30am-11.30pm; 🖋; 🚊1, 2; Ⓤ Schwedenplatz)

HELEN CATHCART/LONELY PLANET ©

Conducting a virtual orchestra at Haus der Musik

Huth Gastwirtschaft   AUSTRIAN €€

5 Map p46, C7

One of several local neo-*Beisln* in this under-the-radar part of Innere Stadt, Huth serves superb Viennese classics such as *Wiener Schnitzel* with cranberry sauce and parsley potatoes, *Selchfleisch* (smoked pork with sauerkraut) and desserts including *Topfenstrudel* (quark-filled strudel), in a high-ceilinged main dining room and vaulted brick cellar, as well as a terrace in summer. Tram to Weihburggasse. (☑01-513 56 44; www.zum-huth.at; 01, Schellinggasse 5; mains €13.90-18.90; ☺noon-11pm; ☒2)

Beim Czaak   BISTRO €€

6 Map p46, D4

In business since 1926, Beim Czaak retains a genuine and relatively simple interior, entered via the restaurant's tree-shaded, ivy-clad courtyard garden. Classic Viennese meat dishes dominate the menu, with long-time favourites including schnitzels (gluten-free variations available), *Tafelspitz* (boiled prime beef), beef goulash with bacon and shredded dumplings, and fried Styrian chicken. Midweek lunch menus cost €9.90. (☑01-513 72 15; www.czaak.com; 01, Postgasse 15; mains €11-18.90; ☺11am-midnight Mon-Sat; ☒1, 2, ⓊSchwedenplatz)

Local Life
Viennese Honey

Some 5000 bee colonies and 600 beekeepers harvest honey within Vienna's city limits, including on the rooftops of the Rathaus, Staatsoper and several hotels. The fruits of their labour are sold at specialist honey boutique **Wald & Wiese** (Map p46, C4; www.waldundwiese.at; 01, Wollzeile 19; ☉9.30am-6.30pm Mon-Fri, 9am-5pm Sat; UStephansplatz), along with honey-based beverages (mead, honey-and-whisky liqueur and grappa), beeswax candles, hand creams, toothpaste, royal jelly...

Café Korb   AUSTRIAN €

7 | Map p46, A4

Famed for its *Apfelstrudel* (apple strudel), Sigmund Freud's former hangout is first and foremost a coffee house, but its top-notch Austrian menu places it in the realm of a *Beisl*. The food is classic – including three house-speciality schnitzels, several varieties of *Würstel* (sausages) – and the crowd eclectic and offbeat. (www.cafekorb.at; 01, Brandstätte 9; mains €5.80-9.80; ☉8am-midnight Mon-Sat, 10am-midnight Sun; 🛜; UStephansplatz)

Donuteria   SWEETS, BAKERY €

8 | Map p46, B7

Inspired Austrian-flavoured doughnuts at this spiffing new shop include *Apfelstrudel*, the Sacher (chocolate and apricot jam, based on the classic *Sacher Torte*), Styrian (pumpkinseed and hazelnut), Mohn (poppyseed and lemon) and the Mozart (pistachio, marzipan and chocolate), based on the *Mozartkugel*, first created in 1890. Tram to Schwarzenbergplatz. (www.donuteria.com; 01, Seilerstätte 30; doughnuts €2.50-5; ☉9.30am-7pm Mon-Fri, 11am-6pm Sat, noon-5pm Sun; 🛜; 🚊2, 71)

Figlmüller   AUSTRIAN €€

9 | Map p46, C4

Vienna would simply be at a loss without Figlmüller. This famous *Beisl* has a rural decor and some of the biggest (on average 30cm in diameter) and best schnitzels in the business. Wine is from the owner's vineyard, but no beer is served. Its popularity has spawned a second location nearby on **Bäckerstrasse** (📞01-512 17 60; 01, Bäckerstrasse 6; ☉11.30am-11.30pm) with a wider menu (and drinks list). (📞01-512 61 77; www.figlmueller.at; 01, Wollzeile 5; mains €9.50-20.50; ☉11am-9.30pm; 🛜; UStephansplatz)

Motto am Fluss   INTERNATIONAL €€

10 | Map p46, D2

Located inside the Wien-City ferry terminal, with dazzling views of the Danube Canal, this restaurant serves Austro-international cuisine with quality organic meats (vegetarian and vegan options available). Its upstairs cafe does great all-day breakfasts, cakes and pastries, and its bar is a superbly relaxed hangout for Austrian wines, beers and house-creation cocktails. (📞01-252 55 10; www.mottoamfluss.at; 01, Franz-Josefs-Kai 2; restaurant mains €13-30, cafe dishes

Understand

The Jews of Vienna

Historically, Vienna has had an ambivalent relationship with its Jewish population, who first settled in the city in 1194. By 1400 they numbered about 800, mostly living in the Jewish quarter centred on a synagogue on Judenplatz.

In 1420 the Habsburg ruler Albrecht V issued a pogrom against the Jews, who later drifted back into the city and prospered until the arrival of bigoted Leopold I and his even more bigoted wife, Margarita Teresa, who blamed her miscarriages on Jews. In 1670 Jews were expelled from the city and their synagogue destroyed, but this weakened the financial strength of Vienna, and the Jewish community was invited back.

The following centuries saw Jews thrive under relatively benign conditions and in the 19th century they were given equal civil rights and prospered in the fields of art and music. The darkest chapter in Vienna's Jewish history began on 12 March 1938 when the Nazis occupied Austria; with them came persecution and curtailment of Jewish civil rights. Businesses were confiscated (including some of Vienna's better-known coffee houses) and Jews were banned from public places; they were obliged to wear a Star of David and go by the names of 'Sara' and 'Israel'. Violence exploded on the night of 9 November 1938 with the November Pogrom, when synagogues and prayer houses were burned – the **Stadttempel** (☏ 01-531 041 11; www.ikg-wien.at; 01, Seitenstettengasse 4; tours adult/child €5/free; ⏲ guided tours 11.30am & 2pm Mon-Thu; Ⓤ Stephansplatz, Schwedenplatz) was the sole surviving synagogue – and 6500 Jews were arrested. Of the 180,000 Jews living in Vienna before the *Anschluss* (annexation), more than 100,000 managed to emigrate before the borders were closed in May 1939; another 65,000 died in ghettos or concentration camps; the steel-and-concrete **Holocaust-Denkmal** (01, Judenplatz; Ⓤ Stephansplatz) built in 2000 is a memorial to those who perished. Only 6000 Jews survived to see liberation by Allied troops.

Most survivors left afterwards. Today the city's Jewish population is approximately 7000 people, including many who immigrated from Eastern Europe and Russia. The website Jewish News from Austria (www.jewishnews.at) is an excellent resource on contemporary Jewish life in Vienna.

€4-10.30; ⊙restaurant 11.30am-2.30pm
& 6pm-midnight, cafe 8am-10pm, bar 6pm-
4am; 🛜🅿; 🚃1, 2, Ⓤschwedenplatz)

Drinking

1516 Brewing Company

MICROBREWERY, PUB

11 🍺 Map p46, B7

Copper vats and bare-brick walls create
an industrial backdrop at this venue
that brews beers from malted wheat,
rye and rice, including unusual varieties, such as Heidi's Blueberry Ale. The
shaded terrace gets packed in summer.
Arrive early for a good seat when it
screens international football (soccer)
games. Tram to Schwarzenbergstrasse.
(🕿01-961 15 16; www.1516brewingcompany.

Ⓠ Local Life

Local Roses

Roses grown by Ingrid Maria Held-
stab in her garden in Vienna's 23rd
district are used in everything from
jams (including spicy versions with
ginger), jellies and liqueurs – which
you can taste in store at **Wiener
Rosenmanufaktur** (Map p46, D4;
www.wienerrosenmanufaktur.at; 01,
Schönlaterngasse 7; ⊙3-7pm Mon-Fri,
11am-5pm Sat Jul & Aug, 1-6.30pm Mon-
Fri, 11am-6.30pm Sat, 2-5pm Sun Sep-Jun;
Ⓤschwedenplatz) – to soaps, aromatic oils and other cosmetics. The
tiny shop occupies the Basilisken-
haus, which dates from 1212.

---

com; 01, Schwarzenbergstrasse 2; ⊙10am-
2am; 🚃2, Ⓤkarlsplatz)

Diglas

CAFE

12 🍷 Map p46, C4

Classic coffee house Diglas has swanky
red-velvet booths, a wide range of coffee
and an elegant clientele. The reputation
of Diglas' cakes precedes it, and the
Apfelstrudel is unrivalled, as are the
seasonal apricot or plum dumplings.
Live piano music fills the room from
7pm to 10pm Thursday to Saturday.
(🕿01-512 57 65; www.diglas.at; 01, Wollzeile 10;
⊙8am-10.30pm; Ⓤstephansplatz)

Zwölf Apostelkeller

PUB

13 🍺 Map p46, C4

Occupying a vast, dimly lit tri-level cellar, historic Zwölf Apostelkeller (Twelve
Apostle Cellar) has a spirited atmosphere bolstered by traditional *Heuriger*
(wine tavern) ballads from 7pm daily.
It offers outstanding local wines and
a good choice of schnapps and beer.
(Twelve Apostle Cellar; 🕿01-512 67 77; www.
zwoelf-apostelkeller.at; 01, Sonnenfelsgasse 3;
⊙11am-midnight; Ⓤstephansplatz)

Entertainment

Jazzland

LIVE MUSIC

14 ⭐ Map p46, C2

Buried in a former wine cellar beneath
Ruprechtskirche, Jazzland is Vienna's
oldest jazz club, dating back nearly
50 years. The music covers the whole

jazz spectrum, and features both local and international acts. Past performers have included Ray Brown and Max Kaminsky. (📞01-533 25 75; www.jazzland. at; 01, Franz-Josefs-Kai 29; cover €11-20; 🕐7pm-2am Mon-Sat mid-Aug–mid-Jul, live music from 9pm; 🚋1, 2, Ⓤ Schwedenplatz)

Shopping

Altmann & Kühne   CHOCOLATE
15 🔒 Map p46, A5

Behind a modernist facade designed by Josef Hoffmann (a founding member of the visual arts collective Wiener Werkstätte), this charming shop is the flagship of century-old chocolatier Altmann & Kühne, which produces handmade chocolates and sweets. Hoffmann also designed the interior and the iconic packaging: miniature hat boxes, luggage trunks, bookshelves and even baroque buildings. (www.altmann-kuehne. at; 01, Graben 30; 🕐9am-6.30pm Mon-Fri, 10am-5pm Sat; Ⓤ Stephansplatz)

Runway   FASHION & ACCESSORIES
16 🔒 Map p46, A4

Runway is a launching pad for up-and-coming Austrian fashion designers, whose creations sit alongside those of their established compatriots. Set over two floors, the chandelier-lit space showcases the direction of womenswear in Vienna and Austria today through its rotating racks of clothes and accessories, as well as through its regular free catwalk shows (check the

online calendar for dates). (www.runway-vienna.at; 01, Goldschmiedgasse 10; 🕐11am-6.30pm Tue-Fri, to 6pm Sat; Ⓤ Stephansplatz)

So Austria   HOMEWARES, FASHION & ACCESSORIES
17 🔒 Map p46, C4

Founded by two South Tyroleans with a passion for Austrian home and fashion accessories, this high-quality shop only sells goods handcrafted in Austria: hand towels, tea towels, bags, shoes, jewellery, sculptures, hats, scarves and clothing. (www.so-austria.at; 01, Lugeck 3a; 🕐10am-7pm Mon-Fri, to 6pm Sat; Ⓤ Stephansplatz)

Explore

Museum District

Showstopping attractions in this cultural neighbourhood include the incomparable Kunsthistorisches Museum, packed with Old Masters; the MuseumsQuartier's cache of museums, cafes, restaurants, bars and performance spaces; and the Renaissance-style Burgtheater. To the west, hip Neubau is an incubator for Vienna's vibrant fashion, art and design scenes.

The Sights in a Day

☀ The baroque imperial stables have cantered into the 21st century with their transformation into the **MuseumsQuartier** (p62), a colossal complex of on-the-pulse bars, cafes, boutiques and museums, including the **Leopold** (p63), the proud holder of the world's largest Schiele collection. Atop the Leopold, **Café Leopold** (p63) is ideal for lunch.

☀ Just around the corner on Maria-Theresien-Platz (pictured left) is the **Kunsthistorisches Museum** (p56), an epic and exhilarating journey through art, where Rubens originals star alongside Giza treasures. Its architectural twin is the neoclassical **Naturhistorisches Museum** (p66) opposite.

☾ When you've had your fill of art and culture, keep tabs on Vienna's evolving fashion and design scene with a mosey around Neubau's backstreet studios and boutiques, before dinner and drinks at the **Brickmakers Pub & Kitchen** (p74).

For a local's day in the Museum District, see p68.

◉ Top Sights

Kunsthistorisches Museum (p56)

MuseumsQuartier (p62)

Naturhistorisches Museum (p66)

○ Local Life

Neubau's Design Scene (p68)

♥ Best of Vienna

Food

Glacis Beisl (p74)

Drinking & Nightlife

Brickmakers Pub & Kitchen (p74)

Siebensternbräu (p75)

Architecture

Rathaus (p72)

Getting There

Ⓤ **U-Bahn** Useful U-Bahn stops include Museumsquartier and Volkstheater on the U2 line. The U3 Neubaugasse and Zieglergasse stops are handy for Neubau.

🚃 **Tram** Trams D, 1, 2 and 71 travel around the Ringstrasse. The No 49 line trundles from Dr-Karl-Renner-Ring through Neubau.

Top Sights
Kunsthistorisches Museum

The Habsburgs built many a bombastic palace but, artistically speaking, the Kunsthistorisches Museum (KHM, Museum of Art History) is their magnum opus. Occupying a neoclassical building as sumptuous as the art it contains, the museum takes you on a time-travel treasure hunt – from classical Rome to Egypt and the Renaissance.

◎ Map p70, H3

www.khm.at

01, Maria-Theresien-Platz

adult/child incl Neue Burg museums €15/free

⏲ 10am–6pm Fri-Wed, to 9pm Thu Jun–Aug, closed Mon Sep–May

Ⓤ Museumsquartier, Volkstheater

Main Entrance

As you climb the ornate main staircase of the Kunsthistorisches Museum, your gaze is drawn to the ever-decreasing circles of the cupola. Marble columns guide the eye to delicately frescoed vaults, roaring lions and Antonio Canova's mighty statue of *Theseus Defeating the Centaur* (1805). Austrian legends Hans Makart and the brothers Klimt have left their hallmark between the columns and above the arcades – the former with lunette paintings, the latter with gold-kissed depictions of women inspired by Greco-Roman and Egyptian art.

Picture Gallery

The Kunsthistorisches Museum's vast Picture Gallery is by far and away the most impressive of its collections. Devote at least an hour or two to exploring its feast of Old Master paintings.

Dutch, Flemish & German Painting

First up in this collection is the **German Renaissance**, where Lucas Cranach the Elder stages an appearance with engaging Genesis tableaux like *Paradise* (1530) and *Fall of Man* (aka *Adam and Eve*; 1537). The key focus is the prized Dürer collection. Dürer's powerful compositions, sophisticated use of light and deep feeling for his subjects shine through in masterful pieces like *Portrait of a Venetian Lady* (1505).

Rubens throws in the deep end of **Flemish baroque** painting next, with paintings rich in Counter-Reformation themes and mythological symbolism. The monumental *Miracle of St Francis Xavier* (1617) and the celestial *The Annunciation* (1610) reveal the iridescent quality and linear clarity that underscored Rubens' style. Mythological masterworks move from the gory, snake-riddled *Medusa* (1617) to the ecstatic celebration of love *Feast of Venus* (1636).

☑ **Top Tips**

▶ Pick up an audio guide and a floor plan in the entrance hall to orientate yourself.

▶ Skip to the front of the queue by booking your ticket online.

▶ Visit between 6pm and 9pm on Thursday for fewer crowds.

▶ Flash photography is not permitted.

✗ **Take a Break**

A meal under the dome is unforgettable. The Kunsthistorisches Museum runs gourmet evenings (6.30pm to 10pm Thursday; adult/child €44/25 excluding museum admission and drinks), and also serves breakfast (10am to 12.30pm; per person €19.90 excluding admission). You're free to wander through the museum to admire the artworks between courses.

In 16th- and 17th-century **Dutch Golden Age** paintings, the desire to faithfully represent reality through an attentive eye for detail and compositional chiaroscuro is captured effortlessly in works by Rembrandt, Ruisdael and Vermeer. Rembrandt's perspicuous *Self-Portrait* (1652), showing the artist in a humble painter's smock, Ruisdael's palpable vision of nature in *The Large Forest* (1655) and Vermeer's seductively allegorical *The Art of Painting* (1665), showing Clio, Greek muse of history, in the diffused light of an artist's studio, are all emblematic of the age.

The final three rooms are an ode to the art of Flemish baroque master **Van Dyck** and Flemish Renaissance painter **Pieter Bruegel the Elder**. Van Dyck's keenly felt devotional works include the *Vision of the Blessed Herman* (1630) and *Madonna and Child with St Rosalie, Peter and Paul* (1629). An entire room is given over to Pieter Bruegel the Elder's vivid depictions of Flemish life and landscapes, alongside his biblical star attraction – *The Tower of Babel* (1563).

Italian, Spanish & French Painting

The first three rooms in its collection of Italian, Spanish and French paintings are given over to key exponents of the **16th-century Venetian** style: Titian, Veronese and Tintoretto. High on your artistic agenda here should be Titian's *Nymph and Shepherd* (1570), elevating the pastoral to the mythological in its portrayal of the futile desire of the flute-playing shepherd for the beautiful maiden out of his reach. Veronese's dramatic depiction of the suicidal Roman heroine *Lucretia* (1583) and Tintoretto's *Susanna at her Bath* (1556) are other highlights.

Devotion is central to Raphael's *Madonna of the Meadow* (1506) in room 4, one of the true masterpieces of the **High Renaissance**, just as it is to the *Madonna of the Rosary* (1601), a stirring Counter-Reformation altarpiece by **Italian baroque** artist Caravaggio in the next room. Room 7 is also a delight, with compelling works like Giuseppe Arcimboldo's anthropomorphic paintings inspired by the seasons and elements. Look out, too, for Venetian landscape painter Canaletto's *Schönbrunn* (1761), meticulously capturing the palace back in its imperial heyday.

Of the artists represented in the final rooms dedicated to **Spanish, French and English** painting, the undoubted star is Spanish court painter Velázquez. Particularly entrancing is his almost 3D portrait of *Infanta Margarita Teresa in a Blue Dress* (1673), a vision of voluminous silk and eight-year-old innocence. Gainsborough's *Suffolk Landscape* (1748), with its feather-light brushwork and suffused colours, and French baroque painter Nicolas Poussin's turbulent *Destruction of the Temple in Jerusalem* (1639) also demand attention.

Kunstkammer

Imagine the treasures you could buy with brimming coffers and the world at your fingertips. The Habsburgs did just that, filling their *Kunstkammer*

A tourist admires art by Rubens

(cabinet of art and curiosities) with an encyclopaedic collection of the rare and the precious. Its 20 themed rooms containing 2200 artworks open a fascinating window on the obsession with collecting curios in royal circles in Renaissance and baroque times.

The biggest crowd-puller here is Benvenuto Cellini's allegorical **Saliera** (salt cellar), commissioned by Francis I of France in 1540. Among the Kunst-kammer's other top-drawer attractions are the wildly expressive, early 17th-century ivory sculpture **Furie** (Master of the Furies), the serenely beautiful **Krumauer Madonna** (1400) and Gasparo Miseroni's lapis lazuli **Dragon Cup** (1570).

Egyptian & Near Eastern Collection

Decipher the mysteries of Egyptian civilisations with a chronological romp through this miniature Giza of a ground-floor collection, beginning with **predynastic** and **Old Kingdom** treasures. Here the exceptionally well-preserved **Offering Chapel of Ka-ni-nisut** spells out the life of the high-ranking 5th-dynasty official in reliefs and hieroglyphs. The Egyptian fondness for nature and adornment finds expression in the artefacts on display here.

Stele, sacrificial altar slabs, jewellery boxes, sphinx busts and pharaoh statues bring to life the **Middle**

First Floor

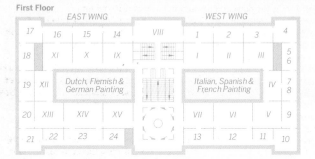

EAST WING

17	16	15	14
18	XI	X	IX
19	XII	Dutch, Flemish & German Painting	
20	XIII	XIV	XV
21	22	23	24

VIII

WEST WING

1	2	3	4
I	II	III	5 6
Italian, Spanish & French Painting		IV	7 8
VII	VI	V	9
13	12	11	10

Ground Floor

WEST WING
Greek & Roman Antiquities

EAST WING

XXV	XXIV	XXII	XX
XXVI			
	Administration		
XXVII	Kunstkammer Wien (Cabinet of Curiosities)		
XXVIII	XXXI	XXXV	XXXVII
	XXXIII		
XXIX	XXX	XXXIV	XXXVI
	XXXII		

XIX

XVIII	XVII	XVI	XV	XIV	XIII
					XII
	Administration				XI
	II	III	IV	VI	VIA	X
	I	V	VII	VIII	IX

Egyptian & Near Eastern Collection

Kingdom and **New Kingdom**. The **Late Period** dips into the land of the pharaohs, at a time when their rule swung from Egypt to Persia. Scout out the 3000-year-old *Book of the Dead of Chonsu-mes,* the polychrome mummy board of Nes-pauti-taui and Canopic jars with lids shaped like monkey, falcon and jackal heads.

Stone sarcophagi, gilded mummy masks and busts of priests and princes transport you back to the **Ptolemaic** and **Greco-Roman** period. In the **Near Eastern** collection, the representation of a prowling lion from Babylon's triumphal Ishtar Gate (604–562 BC) is the big attraction.

Greek & Roman Antiquities

This rich repository reveals the imperial scope for collecting classical antiquities, with 2500 objects traversing three millennia from the Cypriot Bronze Age to early medieval times.

Cypriot and Mycenaean Art catapults you back to the dawn of western civilisation, 2500 years ago. The big draw here is the precisely carved votive statue of a man wearing a finely pleated tunic. Among the muses, torsos and mythological statuettes in **Greek Art** is a fragment from the Parthenon's northern frieze showing two bearded men. The arts flourished in **Hellenistic** times, evident in exhibits like the *Amazonian Sarcophagus*, engraved with warriors so vivid you can almost hear their battle cries. In **pre-Roman Italy**, look for sculptures of Athena, funerary crowns intricately wrought

from gold, and a repoussé showing the Titans doing battle with the Gods.

The sizeable **Roman** stash includes the 4th-century AD *Theseus Mosaic* from Salzburg, a polychrome, geometric marvel recounting the legend of Theseus. You'll also want to take in the captivating 3rd-century AD *Lion Hunt* relief and the 1st-century AD *Gemma Augustea*. Early medieval show-stoppers include the shimmering golden vessels from the **Treasure of Nagyszentmiklós**, unearthed in 1799 in what is now Romania.

Coin Collection

A piggy bank of gigantic Habsburg proportions, this coin collection is one of the world's best. Covering three halls and three millennia on the third floor, the 2000 notes, coins and medallions on display are just a tiny fraction of the Kunsthistorisches Museum's 700,000-piece collection.

The coin collection's first hall presents medals of honour, first used in Renaissance Italy around 1400, and showcases gold and silver House of Habsburg wonders. The second hall travels through monetary time, from the birth of the coin in Lydia in the 7th century BC to the 20th century. Look out for classical coins, like the stater embellished with a lion head, in circulation under Alyattes, King of Lydia (619–560 BC), and Athenian coins featuring the goddess Athena and her pet owl. The third hall stages one-off exhibitions.

Top Sights
MuseumsQuartier

Baroque heritage and the avant-garde collide at the MuseumsQuartier, one of the world's most ambitious cultural spaces. Spanning 90,000 sq metres, this ensemble of museums, cafes, restaurants, shops, bars and performing arts venues occupies the former imperial stables designed by Fischer von Erlach in 1725. You can't see it all in a day, so selectively is the way to go.

👁 Map p70, G4

Museum Quarter; MQ

www.mqw.at

07, Museumsplatz

⌄ information & ticket centre 10am-7pm

Ⓤ Museumsquartier, Volkstheater

Leopold Museum

The **Leopold Museum** (www.leopoldmuseum.org; adult/child €13/8; ⊙10am-6pm Fri-Wed, to 9pm Thu Jun-Aug, 10am-6pm Wed & Fri-Mon, to 9pm Thu Sep-May) is named after Rudolf Leopold, a Viennese ophthalmologist who, on buying his first Egon Schiele (1890–1918) for a song as a young student in 1950, started to amass a huge private collection of mainly 19th-century and modernist Austrian artworks. In 1994 he sold the lot – 5266 paintings – to the Austrian government for €160 million (sold individually, the paintings would have made him €574 million) and the Leopold Museum was born. **Café Leopold** (www.cafe-leopold.at; ⊙10am-midnight Sun-Wed, to 4am Thu, to 6am Fri & Sat; 🛜) is located on the top floor.

The Leopold has a white limestone exterior, open space and natural light flooding most rooms. Considering Rudolf Leopold's love of Schiele, it's no surprise the museum contains the world's largest collection of the painter's work: 41 paintings and 188 drawings and graphics. Among the standouts are the ghostly *Self Seer II Death and Man* (1911), the mournful *Mother with Two Children* (1915) and the caught-in-the-act *Cardinal and Nun* (1912).

Other artists well represented include Albin Egger-Lienz, with his unforgiving depictions of pastoral life, Richard Gerstl and Austria's third-greatest expressionist, Kokoschka. Of the handful of works on display by Klimt, the unmissable is the allegorical *Death and Life* (1910), a swirling amalgam of people juxtaposed by a skeletal grim reaper. Works by Loos, Hoffmann, Otto Wagner, Waldmüller and Romako are also on display.

MUMOK

The dark basalt edifice and sharp corners of **MUMOK** (Museum Moderner Kunst; Museum of Modern Art; www.mumok.at; adult/child €11/free; ⊙2-7pm Mon, 10am-7pm Tue, Wed & Fri-Sun, 10am-9pm Thu; 🚇49 Volkstheater)

☑ Top Tips

▸ Combined tickets are available from the **MQ Point** (☎01-523 58 81-17 31; www.mqpoint.at; ⊙10am-7pm).

▸ The MQ Kombi Ticket (€32) includes entry into every museum (Zoom only has a reduction) and a 30% discount on performances in the TanzQuartier Wien.

▸ The MQ Art Ticket (€26) gives admission into the Leopold Museum, MUMOK, Kunsthalle and reduced entry into Zoom, plus a 30% discount on the TanzQuartier Wien.

✗ Take a Break

Relax at the area's most relaxed cafe/bar, **Kantine** (☎01-523 82 39; www.mq-kantine.at; mains €8.50-13.50; ⊙kitchen 11am-midnight, bar 9am-2am; 🛜 ✐).

Kunsthall eatery **Halle** (☎01-523 70 01; www.die-halle.at; mains €8.50-18.90, 2-course lunch menus €8.90-9.90; ⊙kitchen 10am-midnight, bar to 2am; 🛜 ✐) offers international cuisine.

are a complete contrast to the MQ's historical sleeve. MUMOK is crawling with Vienna's finest collection of 20th- and 21st-century art, centred on fluxus, nouveau realism, pop art and photo-realism. The best of expressionism, cubism, minimal art and Viennese Actionism is represented in a collection of 9000 works rotated and exhibited by theme – but take note that sometimes all this Actionism is packed away to make room for temporary exhibitions.

Viennese Actionism evolved in the 1960s as a radical leap away from mainstream art in what some artists considered to be a restrictive cultural and political climate. Artists like Günter Brus, Otto Mühl, Hermann Nitsch and Rudolf Schwarzkogler aimed to shock with their violent, stomach-churning performance and action art, which often involved using the human body as a canvas. They were successful: not only did their work shock, some artists were even imprisoned for outraging public decency. Other well-known artists represented throughout the museum – Picasso, Paul Klee, René Magritte, Max Ernst and Alberto Giacometti – are positively tame in comparison. Check the program before visiting with children to ensure exhibits are suitable.

Kunsthalle

The **Kunsthalle** (Arts Hall; ☏ 01-521 890; www.kunsthallewien.at; both halls adult/child €12/free; ⊙ 11am-7pm Fri-Wed, to 9pm Thu; 🚇 49 Volkstheater) is a collection of exhibition halls used to showcase local and international contemporary art. Its high ceilings, open planning and

functionality have helped the venue leapfrog into the ranks of the top exhibition spaces in Europe. Programs, which run for three to six months, rely heavily on photography, video, film, installations and new media. Weekend visits include one-hour guided tours in English and German. The Saturday tours (Halle 1 at 3pm, Halle 2 at 4pm) focus on a theme, while Sunday tours (same times) give an overview.

Architekturzentrum Wien

The **Architekturzentrum Wien** (Vienna Architecture Centre; ☏ 01-522 31 15; www.azw.at; exhibition prices vary, library admission free; ⊙ architecture centre 10am-7pm, library 10am-5.30pm Mon, Wed & Fri, to Sat & Sun, closed Thu; 🚇 49 Volkstheater) encompasses three halls used for temporary exhibitions, a library and a cafe. Exhibitions focus on international architectural developments and change regularly. The library is open to the public. The centre also organises regular walking tours through Vienna on Sunday (in German), covering various architectural themes. You need to book ahead; see the website for dates and prices.

Zoom

Kids love this hands-on **children's museum** (☏ 01-524 79 08; www.kindermuseum.at; exhibition adult/child €4/free, activities child €4-6, accompanying adult free; ⊙ 12.45-5pm Tue-Sun Jul & Aug, 8.30am-4pm Tue-Fri, 9.45am-4pm Sat & Sun Sep-Jun, activity times vary) an arts-and-crafts session with lots of play thrown in. Budding Picassos have the chance to make, break, draw, explore and be creative in the 'Atelier'. 'Exhibi-

MUSEUMSQUARTIER COMPLEX

tion' stages a new exhibition every six months, while 'Ocean' appeals to tots with its mirrored tunnels, grottoes and ship deck for adventure play that stimulates coordination. For children aged eight to 14, there is an animated film studio and the future-focused Lab Club. Activities last about 1½ hours and spots can be reserved from the ticket office or by booking online.

Children's Theatre

Dschungel Wien (☎01-522 07 20; www. dschungelwien.at; adult/child tickets from €6/4.50; ☺box office 2.30-6.30pm Mon-Fri, 4.30-6.30pm Sat & Sun) covers the entire spectrum, from drama and puppetry to music, dance and narrative theatre. There are several performances daily in German and occasionally in English; see the website for details. Adults pay kid's prices for matinee performances.

MuseumsQuartier Courtyards

The courtyards host a winter and summer program of events, from film festivals to Christmas markets, literary readings to DJ nights; see the website for details. They are also a popular hangout in the summer months when the cafe terraces hum with life. Two of the most coveted hangouts are Kantine (p63) and Halle (p63).

Top Sights
Naturhistorisches Museum

Vienna's astounding Naturhistorisches Museum (Museum of Natural History) covers four billion years of natural history in a blink. With its exquisitely stuccoed halls and eye-catching cupola, this late 19th-century building is the identical twin of the Kunsthistorisches Museum, which sits opposite. Among its minerals, fossils and dinosaur bones are one-of-a-kind finds like the miniscule 25,000-year-old Venus von Willendorf and a peerless 1100-piece meteorite collection.

◉ Map p70, G3

www.nhm-wien.ac.at

01, Maria-Theresien-Platz

adult/child €10/free, rooftop tours €8

🕙 9am-6.30pm Thu-Mon, to 9pm Wed, rooftop tours in English 3pm Fri, Sat & Sun

Ⓤ Museumsquartier, Volkstheater

Ground Floor: Meteorites, Dinosaurs & Prehistoric Finds

The ground floor leads in with a treasure chest of minerals, fossils and gemstones.

Room 5 blasts you into outer space with the world's largest **meteorite** collection.

For kids and **dinosaur** fans, the big-hitters hang out in room 10 on the ground floor. On a raised platform loom the skeletons of a *Diplodocus, Iguanodon* and a 6m-tall animatronic replica of an *Allosaurus*. Keep an eye out, too, for the skeleton of an *Archelon ischyros,* the largest turtle ever.

Rooms 11 to 13 spell out **prehistory** in artefacts, with curiosities such as the coat of a woolly mammoth and Neanderthal tools.

Occupying rooms 14 to 15, the **anthropological collection**, which reopened in January 2013, brings to life hominid evolution and themes such as bipedalism and brain development at hands-on stations. You can determine the gender, age and cause of death of a virtual skeleton at the CSI table, take and email a prehistoric photo of yourself and spot the difference between Neanderthals and *Homo sapiens* by touching skulls.

First Floor: Zoology

The first floor is a taxidermist's dream. Spotlighting zoology and entomology, the collection slithers, rattles, crawls, swims and swings with common, endangered and extinct species, from single-cell organisms to large mammals. Showstoppers include a 1.4m-long giant clam in room 23, a 5.5m Amazonian anaconda in room 27, a Galapagos giant tortoise in room 28 and two-toed sloths, found in 1831 in Brazil, in room 33.

☑ Top Tip

▶ Panoramic rooftop tours take you onto the building's roof to view the ornate architecture up-close; children under 12 aren't allowed.

✕ Take a Break

Experience quintessential Viennese coffee house culture at grande-dame Café Central (p34).

Tuck into an organic burger from Die Burgermacher (p74).

Local Life
Neubau's Design Scene

The ultimate place to tap into Vienna's burgeoning fashion and design scene is the happening 7th district, Neubau, a hotbed of creativity where you'll often see artisans at work. This half-day stroll takes you to boutiques showcasing creations by the city's most exciting designers, ateliers and fashion-focused cafes. For the inside scoop, visit www.7tm.at.

1 Coffee & Shopping

Das Möbel (http://dasmoebel.at; 07, Burggasse 10; ⊙2pm–midnight Mon–Fri, 10am–midnight Sat & Sun; Ⓤ Volkstheater) showcases some of the most original furniture in Vienna by local artists and designers; it is all for sale.

2 The Workbench

Furniture, lamps, graphic art, even bicycles are among the creations you might find on display at **Die Werkbank**

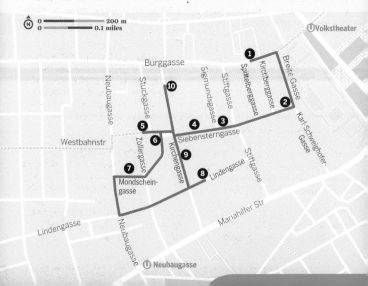

(www.werkbank.cc; 07, Breite Gasse 1; ☺noon-6.30pm Tue-Fri, 11am-5pm Sat; [U]Volkstheater) (The Workbench), an all-white space that operates as a design collective.

❸ Experimental Fashion

The women's casual pieces at **Wiener Konfektion** (www.wienerkonfektion.at; 07, Siebensterngasse 20; ☺12.30-6.30pm Wed-Fri, noon-5pm Sat; 🚌49 Siebensterngasse) are made by experimental owner/designer Maria Fürnkranz-Fielhauer, who uses contemporary fabrics, denim and wool blends but especially vintage '60s and '70s fabrics to create all kinds of pieces.

❹ Art Deco & Bauhaus Designs

Holzer Galerie (www.galerieholzer.at; 07, Siebensterngasse 32; ☺10am-noon & 2-6pm Mon-Fri, to 5pm Sat; 🚌49 Siebensterngasse, [U]Neubaugasse) offers high-quality, polished furniture, ornaments, lighting and art mainly from the art deco and Bauhaus periods, plus easier-to-transport art deco–inspired jewellery.

❺ Handcrafted Bags

Understated clutch, shoulder and tote bags, crafted from vegetable-tanned leather by **Ina Kent** (www.inakent.com; 07, Siebensterngasse 50; ☺11am-7pm Mon-Fri, to 6pm Sat; 🚌49 Siebensterngasse, [U]Volkstheater), are coveted by locals. Attached to the boutique is Ina's workshop where you may spot her crafting pieces.

❻ Applied Arts

Schauraum (☎01-676 757 67 00; www.schauraum.at; 07, Siebensterngasse 33; ☺by appointment; 🚌49 Siebensterngasse, [U]Neubaugasse) zooms in on unusual applied arts. Besides cutting-edge tableware and accessories, you'll find Karin Merkl's versatile jumpers, scarves and jackets made from merino wool or silk.

❼ Fashion Forward

A serious designer store in an all-white 480-sq-metre space, **Park** (www.park.co.at; 07, Mondscheingasse 20; ☺10am-7pm Mon-Fri, to 6pm Sat; [U]Neubaugasse) stocks fashion books, magazines, accessories, furnishings and cutting-edge fashion.

❽ Catwalk Trends

Curve-enhancing dresses, separates and swimwear by designer **Elke Freytag** (http://elkefreytag.com; 07, Lindengasse 14; ☺noon-6pm Wed-Fri, 10am-3pm Sat; 🚌49 Siebensterngasse, [U]Neubaugasse) regularly grace catwalks in Vienna and beyond.

❾ Emerging Talent

Forward-looking boutique **S/GHT** (www.sight.at; 07, Kirchengasse 24; ☺11am-6pm Mon-Sat; [U]Neubaugasse) promotes emerging Austrian labels such as Katharina Schmid and Meshit along with breakthrough international designers.

❿ Unique Jewellery

At **Schmuckladen** (http://baustelle.schmuckladen.org/wordpress; 07, Kirchengasse 40; ☺1-6.30pm Wed, 11am-6.30pm Thu & Fri, 11am-5pm Sat; 🚌49 Siebensterngasse, [U]Volkstheater) workshop, goldsmith Ilga puts her own imaginative spin on jewellery, from fragile silver-leaf necklaces to quirky button rings.

For reviews see

👁 Top Sights   p56
◉ Sights   p72
✖ Eating   p73
🍷 Drinking   p74
🔒 Shopping   p75

Florianigasse

Josefstädter Str Ⓤ

Josefstädter Str

Schönborn-gasse

Lerchenfelder Gürtel

Thaliastr

Stolzenthalergasse

Pfeilgasse

Lerchengasse

Lerchenfelder Gürtel

Lerchenfelder Str

Hasnerstr

Ⓤ

Kaiserstr

Zieglergasse

🔒1

Myrthengasse

Neustiftgasse

Herbststr

Halbgasse

Burggasse

Gablenzgasse

Burggasse Stadthalle Ⓤ

Wimberger

Wurzbach-gasse

Shottenfeldgasse

Bandgasse

Hermanngasse

Kandlgasse

Urban-Loritz-Platz

Märzpark

Kaiserstr

🍷8

Westbahnstr

Hütteldorfer Str

Neubaugürtel

Neubaugürtel

Kenyongasse

Zieglergasse

Märzstr

Löhrgasse

Lindengasse

Andreasgasse

Richte gass

Hofmobiliendepot

3◉

N 0   500 m
   0   0.25 miles

Apollogasse

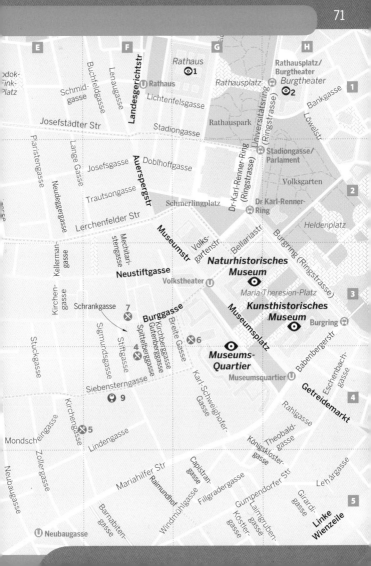

E   F   G   H

odok-
Fink-
Platz

Schmid-
gasse

Buchfeldgasse

Lenaugasse

Landesgerichtstr

Rathaus
⊙1

Rathausplatz/
Burgtheater

Rathausplatz

Burgtheater
⊙2

1

Ⓤ Rathaus

Lichtenfelsgasse

Bankgasse

Löwelstr

Josefstädter Str

Stadiongasse

Rathauspark

Universitätsring (Ringstrasse)

Piaristengasse

Lange Gasse

Neudeggergasse

Josefsgasse

Doblhoffgasse

Auerspergstr

Dr-Karl-Renner-Ring (Ringstrasse)

Ⓤ Stadiongasse/
Parlament

Volksgarten

2

Trautsongasse

Schmerlingplatz

Dr Karl-Renner-
Ⓤ Ring

Lerchenfelder Str

Heldenplatz

Kellermann-
gasse

Mechitari-
stengasse

Museumstr

Volks-
gartenstr

Bellariastr

Burgring (Ringstrasse)

Kirchen-
gasse

Neustiftgasse

Naturhistorisches
Museum
⊙

Volkstheater Ⓤ

Maria-Theresien-Platz

3

Schrankgasse

7
⊗

Burggasse

Kirchberggasse

Breite Gasse

Museumsplatz

Kunsthistorisches
Museum
⊙

Burgring Ⓤ

Stuckgasse

Sigmundsgasse

Stiftgasse

4
⊗

Spittelberggasse

Guttenberggasse

⊗6

Museums-
Quartier
⊙

Babenbergerstr

Eschenbach-
gasse

Siebensterngasse

Museumsquartier Ⓤ

Getreidemarkt

4

Ⓥ 9

Karl-Schweighofer-
Gasse

Rahlgasse

Kirchengasse

⊗5

Lindengasse

Theobald-
gasse

Königskloster-
gasse

Mondscheingasse

Capistran-
gasse

Lambrug-
gasse

Lehárgasse

Zollergasse

Mariahilfer Str

Raimundhof

Windmühlgasse

Fillgradergasse

Gumpendorfer Str

Köstler-
gasse

Girardi-
gasse

Linke
Wienzeile

5

Neubaugasse

Barnabiten-
gasse

Ⓤ Neubaugasse

Sights

Rathaus
LANDMARK

1 ◉ Map p70, G1

The crowning glory of the Ringstrasse boulevard's 19th-century architectural ensemble, Vienna's neo-Gothic City Hall was completed in 1883 by Friedrich von Schmidt of Cologne Cathedral fame and modelled on Flemish city halls. From the fountain-filled **Rathauspark**, where Josef Lanner and Johann Strauss I, fathers of the Viennese waltz, are immortalised in bronze, you get the full effect of its facade of lacy stonework, pointed-arch windows and spindly turrets. One-hour guided tours are in German; multilingual audio guides are free. (www.wien.gv.at; 01, Rathausplatz 1; admission free; ☉tours 1pm Mon, Wed & Fri Sep-Jun, 1pm Mon-Fri Jul & Aug; ⛱D, 1, 2 Rathaus, Ⓤ Rathaus)

☑ Top Tip

Free Guided Tours

Time your visit to catch one of the neighbourhood sights' free guided tours. Gallery tours that won't cost you a cent include those at the Leopold Museum (p63) at 3pm on Sunday, the Kunsthalle Wien (p64) at 3pm and 4pm on Saturday and Sunday, and the MUMOK (p63) (check schedules online). Best of all are the gratis guided tours of the neo-Gothic Rathaus (p72) at 1pm on Monday, Wednesday and Friday.

Burgtheater
THEATRE

2 ◉ Map p70, H1

This stately Renaissance-style theatre (p89) sits with aplomb on the Ringstrasse. Designed by Gottfried Semper and Karl Hasenauer in 1888, it was restored to its pre-WWII glory in 1955. The company dates to 1741, making it Europe's second oldest. If the walls could talk, they'd tell of musical milestones like the premiere of Mozart's *Marriage of Figaro* (1786) and Beethoven's *1st Symphony* (1800). For a behind-the-scenes look at this magnificent theatre, join one of the regular guided tours. (☎01-514 44 4140; www.burgtheater.at; 01, Universitätsring; tours adult/child €7/3.50; ☉tours 3pm Sep-Jun; ⛱D, 1, 2 Rathaus, Ⓤ Rathaus)

Hofmobiliendepot
MUSEUM

3 ◉ Map p70, D5

The Habsburgs stashed away the furniture not displayed in the Hofburg, Schönbrunn, Schloss Belvedere and their other palaces at the Hofmobiliendepot. A romp through this regal attic of a museum, covering four floors and 165,000 objects, provides fascinating insight into furniture design, with highlights such as a display of imperial travelling thrones, Emperor Maximilian's coffin and Empress Elisabeth's neo-Renaissance bed from Gödöllő Castle. One of the more underrated museums in the city, it's included in the Sisi Ticket (p32). (www.hofmobiliendepot.at; 07, Andreasgasse 7; adult/child

KOVERNINSKA OLGA/SHUTTERSTOCK ©

Rathaus

€9.50/6, incl 1-hr tour €11.50/7; ⏱10am-6pm; Ⓤ Neubaugasse)

Eating

Tian Bistro

VEGETARIAN €€

🍴 4 Map p70, F4

Colourful tables set up on the cobbled laneway outside Tian Bistro in summer, while indoors, a glass roof floods the atrium-style, greenery-filled dining room in light. It's the cheaper, more relaxed offspring of Michelin-starred vegetarian restaurant **Tian** (📞01-890 46 65-2; www.taste-tian.com; 01, Himmelpfortgasse 23; 2/3-course lunch menus €29/34, 4-/6-course dinner menus €93/108;

⏱noon-2pm & 5.45-9pm Tue-Sat; 🍴; 🚋2, Ⓤ Stephansplatz), and serves sublime vegetarian and vegan dishes such as black truffle risotto with Piedmont hazelnuts, as well as breakfast until 2pm on weekends. (📞01-890 466 532; www.tian-bistro.com; 07, Schrankgasse 4; mains €10-18; ⏱11.30am-10pm Mon-Fri, 9am-10pm Sat & Sun; 🍴; 🚋49 Siebensterngasse/Stiftgasse, Ⓤ Volkstheater)

Figar

CAFE €

🍴 5 Map p70, E4

Splashed with a street-art-style mural, Neubau's hottest brunch spot serves spectacular breakfasts until 2pm including Working Class Hero (sausage, mushrooms, homemade baked beans, spinach and skewered roast cherry tomatoes) and Chosen (Viennese Thum ham, chorizo, Emmental and scrambled eggs), plus yoghurt, muesli, porridge and pastries. At night it morphs into a craft cocktail bar with a soundtrack of house music. (www.figar.net; 07, Kirchengasse 18; breakfast €5.50-9, mains €10-15; ⏰kitchen 8am-10.30pm Mon-Fri, 9am-4pm Sat & Sun, bar to midnight Sun-Wed, to 2am Thu-Sat; Ⓤ Neubaugasse)

Local Life
Christmas Markets

Vienna's much-loved Christmas market season runs from around mid-November to Christmas Eve. Magical *Christkindlmärkte* set up in streets and squares, with stalls selling wooden toys, holiday decorations and traditional food such as *Wurst* (sausages) and *Glühwein* (mulled wine). The centrepiece is the **Rathausplatz Christkindlmarkt** (Map p70, G1; www.christkindlmarkt.at; ⏰10am-10pm 13 Nov–26 Dec; 🚋D, 1, 2 Rathaus, Ⓤ Rathaus).

Spread over the charming cobblestoned streets of the Spittelberg quarter, the charming **Spittelberg Christkindlmarkt** (Map p70, F3; www.spittelberg.at; 07, Spittelberggasse; ⏰2-9pm Mon-Thu, 2-9.30pm Fri, 10am-9.30pm Sat, 10am-9pm Sun 13 Nov-23 Dec; Ⓤ Volkstheater, Museumsquartier) is traditionally the most beloved by the Viennese.

Glacis Beisl

BISTRO €€

6 🍴 Map p70, G3

Hidden downstairs along Breite Strasse in the MuseumsQuartier (follow the signs from MUMOK), Glacis Beisl does an authentic goulash, an accomplished *Wiener Schnitzel* and some other very decent Austrian classics, which you can wash down with local Viennese reds and whites. In summer, dine beneath the walnut trees among flowering geraniums in the sprawling courtyard. (📞01-526 56 60; http://glacisbeisl.at; 07, Breite Gasse 4; mains €7.60-17.80; ⏰kitchen noon-11pm, bar 11am-2am; 🍴; Ⓤ Volkstheater)

Die Burgermacher

BURGERS €

7 🍴 Map p70, F3

The burgers at this small, alternative joint are made using organic ingredients and include meat and vegetarian options, from halloumi cheese to Mexican varieties. If you can't get a table, grab a spot at the side bench or get takeaway. (www.dieburgermacher.at; 07, Burggasse 12; burgers €8.50-10.50; ⏰5-10.30pm Tue-Fri, noon-10.30pm Sat, noon-9.30pm Sun; 🍴; Ⓤ Volkstheater)

Drinking

Brickmakers Pub & Kitchen

CRAFT BEER

8 🍺 Map p70, D4

British racing-green metro tiles, a mosaic floor and a soundtrack of disco, hip-hop, funk and soul set the scene for brilliant craft beers and ciders: there are 30 on tap at any one time and over 150 by the bottle. Pop-ups take over the kitchen, and at lunch and dinner guest chefs cook anything from gourmet fish and chips to BBQ-smoked beef brisket. (📞01-997 44 14; www.brickmakers.at; 07, Zieglergasse 42; ⏱4pm-2am Mon-Fri, 10am-2am Sat, 10am-1am Sun; Ⓤ Zieglergasse)

Le Troquet
BAR

French is lingua franca at Le Troquet (see 5 ✖ Map p70, E4), which is styled like a Parisian cafe with a zinc bar. Wines and craft beers are sourced from all over France, and cocktails are retro (Harvey Wallbanger, Cuba Libre). Classic French cafe dishes include *croques monsieur* and *madame* (toasted ham and cheese sandwiches, the latter with a fried egg on top). (www.letroquet.at; 07, Kirchengasse 18; ⏱11am-2am Mon-Sat, 5pm-2am Sun; Ⓤ Neubaugasse)

Siebensternbräu
MICROBREWERY

9 🍺 Map p70, F4

Swig some of Vienna's finest microbrews at this lively, no-nonsense brewpub. Besides hoppy lagers and malty ales, there are unusual varieties like hemp, chilli and wood-smoked beer. Try them with pretzels or pub grub like schnitzel, goulash and pork knuckles (lunch mains €6.90, dinner mains €7.50 to €18.90). The courtyard garden fills up quickly in the warmer months. (www.7stern.at; 07, Siebensterngasse 19; ⏱11am-midnight; Ⓤ Neubaugasse)

☑ Top Tip

Discount Theatre Tickets

Tickets at the Burgtheater (p89) and Akademietheater (p111) sell for 75% of their face value an hour before performances.

Standby tickets (€10) for **Vienna's English Theatre** (Map p70, F2; 📞01-402 12 60; www.englishtheatre.at; 08, Josefsgasse 12; tickets €24-47; ⏱box office 10am-7.30pm Mon-Fri, 5-7.30pm Sat performance days mid-Aug–Jun, closed Jul–mid-Aug; 🚋2 Rathaus, Josefstädter Strasse, Ⓤ Rathaus) go on sale 15 minutes before showtime. Productions range from timeless pieces, such as Shakespeare, to contemporary works and comedies.

Shopping

Dirndlherz
CLOTHING

10 🔒 Map p70, D2

Putting her own spin on Alpine fashion, Austrian designer Gabriela Urabl creates one-of-a-kind, high-fashion dirndls, from sassy purple-velvet bosom-lifters to 1950s-style gingham numbers and dirndls emblazoned with quirky motifs like pop-art and punk-like conical metal studs. T-shirts with tag-lines like '*Mei Dirndl is in da Wäsch*' ('My dirndl is in the wash') are also available. (http://dirndlherz.at; 07, Lerchenfelder Strasse 50; ⏱11am-6pm Thu & Fri, to 4pm Sat; Ⓤ Volkstheater)

Explore

Karlsplatz

Fringing the Ringstrasse in the southeast corner of the Innere Stadt, this neighbourhood includes the city's sublime Staatsoper opera house, and extends south beyond Vienna's enormous market and food paradise, Naschmarkt, into some of the city's most interesting *Vorstädte* (inner suburbs), with great eating, drinking, nightlife and Viennese *Vorstadt* character.

The Sights in a Day

☀ Start off at this neighbourhood's magnificent **Karlskirche** (p84), gazing at its baroque frescoes, before checking out extraordinary art including Klimt's exquisitely gilded *Beethoven Frieze* at the seminal **Secession** (p84) museum showcasing works by these pioneering turn-of-the-20th-century artists.

☀ Immerse yourself in the multilingual buzz, street-food sizzle and market-stall banter of the **Naschmarkt** (p91), and deliberate over its sit-down eateries for lunch. Afterwards, head south to the easygoing Freihausviertel and Vienna suddenly shrinks to village scale, with arty cafes, ateliers and food shops run by folk with genuine passion.

☾ Burgers, cheesecake and gin are the specialities of hotspot **Said the Butcher to the Cow** (p86). Night time lifts the curtain on high-calibre opera and classical music in some of the world's finest concert halls, including the incomparable **Staatsoper** (p78), as well as a wealth of lively bars for which this area is renowned, particularly along Gumpendorfer Strasse.

For a local's day in Karlsplatz, see p80.

◉ Top Sights
Staatsoper (p78)

○ Local Life
Epicure Tour of the Freihausviertel (p80)

♥ Best of Vienna

Coffee Houses
Café Sperl (p87)

Food
Zum Alten Fassl (p87)

Vollpension (p85)

Naschmarkt (p91)

Eis Greissler (p86)

Drinking & Nightlife
Sekt Comptoir (p81)

Wieden Bräu (p88)

Getting There

Ⓤ **U-Bahn** Karlsplatz is well connected to all corners of Vienna, served by the U-Bahn lines U1, U2 and U4. The U4 line to Kettenbrückengasse is handy for Naschmarkt and the Freihausviertel, while the U3 line (Zieglergasse, Neubaugasse etc) is useful for reaching Mariahilfer Strasse.

🚊 **Tram** Trams 1 and 62 stop at Karlsplatz and pass through Wieden.

Top Sights
Staatsoper

Built between 1861 and 1869 by August Sicardsburg and Eduard van der Nüll, the Staatsoper initially revolted the Viennese public and Habsburg royalty and quickly earned the nickname 'stone turtle'. Despite the frosty reception, it went on to house some of the most iconic directors in history, including Gustav Mahler, Richard Strauss and Herbert van Karajan.

◉ Map p82, G1

www.wiener-staatsoper.at

01, Opernring 2

🚊 D, 1, 2, 71 Kärntner Ring/Oper, Ⓤ Karlsplatz

Guided Tours

Guided tours take in highlights such as the foyer, graced with busts of Beethoven, Schubert and Haydn and frescoes of celebrated operas, and the main staircase, watched over by marble allegorical statues embodying the liberal arts. The Tea Salon dazzles in 22-carat gold leaf, the Schwind Foyer captivates with 16 opera-themed oil paintings by Austrian artist Moritz von Schwind, while the Gustav Mahler Hall is hung with tapestries inspired by Mozart's *The Magic Flute*. You'll also get a behind-the-scenes look at the stage, which raises the curtain on over 300 performances each year.

Performances

Productions are lavish, formal affairs, where people dress up accordingly. In the interval, wander the foyer and refreshment rooms to fully appreciate the gold-and-crystal interior. Opera is not performed here in July and August (tours still take place). **Tickets** (☎01-514 44 7810; www.bundestheater.at; 01, Operngasse 2; ⏰8am-6pm Mon-Fri, 9am-noon Sat & Sun; ⓊStephansplatz) can be purchased up to two months in advance.

Opernball

Of the 300 or so balls held in January and February, the Opernball (Opera Ball) is number one. Held in the Staatsoper on the Thursday preceding Ash Wednesday, it's a supremely elegant affair, with the men in tails and women in shining white gowns. Tickets range from €490 to an eye-watering €21,000 and sell out years in advance.

☑ **Top Tips**

▶ Guided tours (adult/child €7.50/3.50) in English and German last 40 minutes and generally depart on the hour between 10am and 4pm.

▶ The contents of its former Staatsopernmuseum, which closed in 2014, are now displayed in the TheaterMuseum (p32) near the Hofburg. They include portraits of operatic greats, costumes, stage designs and documents.

✗ **Take a Break**

Burgers are brilliant at nearby Said the Butcher to the Cow (p86).

Grab a *Würstel* (sausage) at cult-status sausage stand, Bitzinger Würstelstand am Albertinaplatz (p25).

Local Life
Epicure Tour of the Freihausviertel

Once home to impoverished artisans, today the Freihausviertel has been revitalised: its attractive lanes harbour boho cafes, speciality food stores and some of Vienna's most exciting new galleries, ateliers and boutiques. After a morning browsing Vienna's gourmand's fantasyland, the Naschmarkt, continue your spin through the 4th district with this foodie tour.

❶ Literary Lunch

'Spices and books for cooks' is the credo of **Babettes** (www.babettes.at; 04, Schleifmühlgasse 17; ⊘10am-7pm Mon-Fri, 10.30am-5pm Sat Sep-Jul, 11am-6pm Mon-Fri, 10am-3pm Aug; Ⓤ Kettenbrückengasse), with a round-the-world tour of cookbooks to browse. On weekdays, a different lunch special (such as curry) sizzles in the open kitchen, prepared with own-brand spices and fresh Naschmarkt produce. Food is

served from noon to 2.30pm Monday to Friday. Evening cookery-class themes range from tapas to Tuscan cuisine.

❷ Austrian Bubbly

Raise a toast at **Sekt Comptoir** (www.sektcomptoir.at; 04, Schleifmühlgasse 19; ⊙5-11pm Mon-Thu, noon-11pm Fri & Sat; Ⓤ Kettenbrückengasse) over a glass of Burgenland Sekt (sparkling wine). As it's located just a few blocks from the Naschmarkt, shoppers with bulging grocery bags often spill onto the sidewalk here.

❸ Sugar & Spice

If you're lucky you'll see the Henzl family drying, grinding and blending their home-grown and foraged herbs and spices with sugar and salt at delightfully old-school **Henzls Ernte** (www.henzls.at; 03, Kettenbrückengasse 3; ⊙1-6pm Tue-Fri, 9am-5pm Sat; Ⓤ Kettenbrückengasse). Specialities include sloe-berry salt, lavender sugar, wild garlic pesto and green tomato preserve.

❹ Farm Fresh

Nip into farmers' store **Helene** (http://bauernladenhelene.at; 05, Kettenbrückengasse 7; ⊙8am-6pm Tue-Fri, to 3pm Sat; Ⓤ Kettenbrückengasse) for a smorgasbord of top-quality regional produce. Besides super-fresh fruit and veg, cheese and meat, you'll find Joseph Brot von Pheinsten organic loaves from the Waldviertel, chestnut, larch and acacia honeys from Lower Austria and wine and chilli jam from Burgenland.

❺ Apple of a Needle's Eye

At dinky workshop-store **Näherei Apfel** (www.naeherei-apfel.at; Kettenbrückengasse 8; ⊙11am-6pm Tue-Fri, 10am-3pm Sat; Ⓤ Kettenbrückengasse), you can buy Burgenland apples dried, preserved, chipped, juiced and by the kilo, browse Ursula's funky sweaters, jersey dresses and bags, or you can learn to sew.

❻ Just Desserts

At chocolatier and pâtisserie **Fruth** (www.fruth.at; 04, Kettenbrückengasse 20; ⊙11am-7pm Tue-Fri, 9am-5pm Sat; Ⓤ Kettenbrückengasse), the inimitable Eduard Fruth creates edible works of art. Deliberate over delicacies including strawberry tartlets, rich truffles, feather-light éclairs, and chocolate flavoured with chilli, chestnut and cranberry.

❼ Afternoon Tea

A boudoir of a French tearoom, **Süssi** (☏01-943 13 24; www.suessi.at; 04, Operngasse 30; desserts €3.50-7, afternoon tea €18; ⊙11am-9pm Tue-Sat, 1-9pm Sun; Ⓤ Karlsplatz) is a real blast from the past with its ruby red chairs, striped wallpaper, lace doilies and candelabras. Brews from Paris-based Mariage Frères are served in proper crockery and go perfectly with the tempting array of macarons, quiches, fruit tarts and cream cakes.

For reviews see

⬤	Top Sights	p78
◉	Sights	p84
✕	Eating	p85
🍷	Drinking	p87
★	Entertainment	p89
🛍	Shopping	p90

0 500 m
0 0.25 miles

Burggasse

Sigmundsgasse
Stiftgasse
Spittelberggasse
Kirchberggasse
Breite Gasse
Karl-Schweighofer-Gasse

Stuckgasse
Neubaugasse
Siebensterngasse
Mondscheingasse
Kirchengasse
Neustiftgasse

Zieglergasse
Shottenfeldgasse
Lindengasse
Zollergasse
Windmühlgasse
Fillgradergasse

Richtergasse
Andreasgasse
Barnabiten-gasse

Neubaugasse Ⓤ
Schadekgasse
Stiegengasse
Joanelligasse
🛍 22

Zieglergasse Ⓤ
Mariahilfer Str
Amerlingstr
Gumpendorfer Str
Dürergasse

Otto-Bauer-Gasse
13 ✕ Esterházygasse
Hamburgerstr
12 🍷

Königasse
Magdalenenstr
🍷 14

Webgasse
Linke Wienzeile
Grün-gasse
Rüdigergasse
Weihrgasse

21 🛍
4 ◉ *Haydnhaus*
Stumpergasse
Liniengasse
Schönbrunner Str
Stroba...gasse

Millergasse
Pilgramgasse Ⓤ
Pilgramgasse
Margareter plat...

Grabnergasse
Mollardgasse
Wien
Rechte Wienzeile

Gumpendorfer Str
Garten-gasse

Sights

Karlskirche
CHURCH

1 ⊙ Map p82, H3

Built between 1716 and 1739, after a vow by Karl VI at the end of the 1713 plague, Vienna's finest baroque church rises at the southeast corner of Resselpark. It was designed and commenced by Johann Bernhard Fischer von Erlach and completed by his son Joseph. The huge elliptical copper dome reaches 72m; the highlight is the lift (elevator) to the cupola (included in admission) for a close-up view of the intricate frescoes by Johann Michael Rottmayr. Audio guides cost €2. (St Charles Church; www.karlskirche.at; 04, Karlsplatz; adult/child €8/free; ⊙9am-6pm Mon-Sat, noon-7pm Sun; Ⓤ Karlsplatz)

Secession
MUSEUM

2 ⊙ Map p82, F2

In 1897, 19 progressive artists swam away from the mainstream Künstlerhaus artistic establishment to form the *Wiener Secession* (Vienna Secession). Among their number were Klimt, Josef Hoffman, Kolo Moser and Joseph M Olbrich. Olbrich designed the new exhibition centre of the Secessionists, which combined sparse functionality with stylistic motifs. Its biggest draw is Klimt's exquisitely gilded *Beethoven Frieze*. Guided tours in English (€3) lasting one hour take place at 11am Saturday. Audio guides cost €3. (www.secession.at; 01, Friedrichstrasse 12; adult/child €9/5.50; ⊙10am-6pm Tue-Sun; Ⓤ Karlsplatz)

Akademie der Bildenden Künste
MUSEUM

3 ⊙ Map p82, F2

Founded in 1692, the Akademie der Bildenden Künste is an often underrated art space. Its gallery concentrates on the classic Flemish, Dutch and German painters, and includes important figures such as Hieronymus Bosch, Rembrandt, Van Dyck, Rubens, Titian, Francesco Guardi and Cranach the Elder, to mention a handful. Hourlong tours (€3, in German only) take place at 10.30am every Sunday. Audio guides cost €2. The supreme highlight is Bosch's impressive and gruesome *Triptych of the Last Judgement* altarpiece (1504–08). (Academy of Fine Arts; www.akbild.ac.at; 01, Schillerplatz 3; adult/child €8/free; ⊙10am-6pm Tue-Sun; 🚊 D, 1, 2 Kärntner Ring/Oper, Ⓤ Museumsquartier, Karlsplatz)

Haydnhaus
MUSEUM

4 ⊙ Map p82, A4

Haydn lived in Vienna during the heady times of Napoleon's occupation, and this exhibition at his last residence focuses on Vienna as well as London during the late 18th and early 19th centuries. An Austrian composer prominent in the classical period, he is most celebrated for his 104 symphonies and 68 string quartets. The small garden here is modelled on the original. Audio guides cost €4. (www.wienmuseum.at; 06, Haydngasse 19; adult/child €5/free; ⊙10am-1pm & 2-6pm Tue-Sun; Ⓤ Zieglergasse)

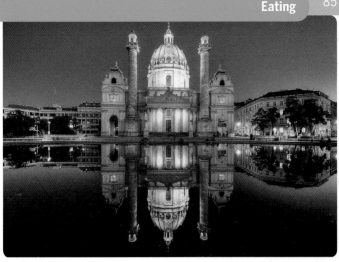

Karlskirche

Stadtbahn Pavillons

NOTABLE BUILDING

5 Map p82, G2

Peeking above the Resselpark at Karlsplatz are two of Otto Wagner's finest designs, the Stadtbahn Pavillons. Built in 1898 at a time when Wagner was assembling Vienna's first public transport system (1893–1902), the pavilions are gorgeous examples of *Jugendstil*, with floral motifs and gold trim on a structure of steel and marble. The west pavilion holds an exhibit on Wagner's most famous *Jugendstil* works, the **Kirche am Steinhof** (📞 910 60-11 204; 14, Baumgartner Höhe 1; tour €8, Art Nouveau tour, including church €12; ⏰ 4-5pm Sat, noon-4pm Sun, tours 3-4pm Sat, 4-5pm

Sun; 🚌 47A, 48A Baumgartner Höhe) and **Postsparkasse** (p45). The eastern pavilion is home to Club U (p88). (www.wienmuseum.at; 04, Karlsplatz; adult/child €5/free; ⏰ 10am-6pm Tue-Sun Apr-Oct; Ⓤ Karlsplatz)

Eating

Vollpension

CAFE €

6 Map p82, F3

This white-painted brick space with mismatched vintage furniture, tasselled lampshades and portraits on the walls is run by 15 *omas* (grandmas) and *opas* (grandpas) along with their families, with more than 200 cakes in their collective repertoire.

Local Life

Organic Ice Cream

The inevitable queue makes **Eis Greissler** (Map p82, D2; www.eis-greissler.at; 06, Mariahilfer Strasse 33; 1/2/3/4/5 scoops €1.50/2.80/3.80/4.80/5.30; ⏱11am-10pm; ⓊMuseumsquartier) easy to spot. Locals flock here whatever the weather for ice cream made from organic milk, yoghurt and cream from its own farm in Lower Austria, and vegans are well catered for with soy and oat milk varieties. All-natural flavours vary seasonally but might include cinnamon, pear, strawberry, raspberry, chocolate, hazelnut or butter caramel.

Breakfast, such as avocado and feta on pumpernickel bread, is served until 4pm; lunch dishes include a vegan goulash with potato and tofu. (www.vollpension.wien; 04, Schleifmühlgasse 16; dishes €2.80-7.90; ⏱9am-10pm Tue-Sat, to 8pm Sun; 🖋; 🚃1, 62 Wien Paulanergasse)

Said the Butcher to the Cow

BURGERS, STEAK €€

7 🍴 Map p82, F1

Not only does this hip hangout have a brilliant name, it serves knock-out brioche-bun burgers (chicken teriyaki with wasabi mayo; black tiger prawns with bok choy; red wine vinegar-marinated halloumi with mango chutney; black bean and guacamole with boletus mushrooms), chargrilled steaks, and house-speciality cheesecakes. Better yet, it moonlights as a gin bar with 30 varieties and seven different tonics. (🕿01-535 69 69; http://butcher-cow.at; 01, Opernring 11; mains €10.80-31.90; ⏱kitchen 5-11pm Tue-Sat, bar 5pm-1am Tue & Wed, 5pm-2am Thu-Sat; 🚃D, 1, 2, 71 Kärnter Ring/Oper, Ⓤ Karlsplatz)

Silberwirt

AUSTRIAN €€

8 🍴 Map p82, E5

This atmospheric neo-*Beisl* offers traditional Viennese cuisine, mostly using organic and/or local produce. A meal might begin with Waldviertel sheep's cheese salad with walnuts and poppy seeds, followed by trout with herby potatoes and almond butter, and *Palatschinken* (pancakes) with homemade apricot jam. A dedicated kids' menu appeals to little appetites. In summer, dine in the tree-shaded garden. (🕿01-544 49 07; www.silberwirt.at; 05, Schlossgasse 21; mains €8-16; ⏱noon-midnight; 👶; Ⓤ Pilgramgasse)

El Burro

STREET FOOD €

9 🍴 Map p82, F3

At this hip Mexican street-food cantina, first choose your base (burritos, tacos, quesadillas and tostada tortilla bowls), then fillings (beef brisket, pulled pork, sweet potato and beets, octopus ceviche) and toppings (tomato salsa, guacamole, corn, spiced mango, sour cream), plus drinks (craft beers, cocktails, homemade lemonades, Austrian wines). There's a handful of tables inside and more on the summer terrace. (www.elburro.at; 04, Margaretenstrasse 9; dishes €7.20-9.60; ⊘11.30am-10pm Mon-Fri, 1-10pm Sat & Sun; 🚋1, 62 Wien Paulanergasse, Ⓤ Taubstummengasse)

Zum Alten Fassl AUSTRIAN €€

10 🍴 Map p82, E5

With its private garden amid residential houses and polished wooden interior, this well-kept *Beisl* is a great spot to sample the Viennese favourites and regional specialities, such as *Eierschwammerl* (chanterelles) and *Blunzengröstl* (a potato, bacon, onion and blood sausage fry-up). When it's in season, *Zanderfilet* (fillet of zander) is the chef's favourite. Midweek lunch menus cost €6.30 to €7.80. (📞01-544 42 98; www.zum-alten-fassl.at; 05, Ziegelofengasse 37; mains €8.90-15.50; ⊘11.30am-3pm & 5pm-midnight Mon-Fri, 5pm-midnight Sat, noon-3pm & 5pm-midnight Sun; Ⓤ Pilgramgasse)

Drinking

Café Sperl COFFEE

11 🚇 Map p82, E2

With its gorgeous *Jugendstil* fittings, grand dimensions, cosy booths and unhurried air, 1880-opened Sperl is one of the finest coffee houses in Vienna. The must-try is *Sperl Torte*, an almond-and-chocolate-cream dream. Grab a slice and a newspaper (over 10 daily in English, French and German), order a coffee (34 kinds), and join the rest of the people-watching patrons. (www.cafesperl.at; 06, Gumpendorfer Strasse 11; ⊘7am-11pm Mon-Sat, 11am-8pm Sun; 📶; Ⓤ Museumsquartier, Kettenbrückengasse)

Café Rüdigerhof CAFE

12 🚇 Map p82, D4

Rüdigerhof's facade is a glorious example of *Jugendstil* architecture, and the '50s furniture and fittings inside could be straight out of an *I Love Lucy* set. The atmosphere is homey and familiar and the wraparound garden huge and shaded. Hearty Austrian fare (huge schnitzels, spinach *Spätzle*, goat's cheese strudel) is way above average. On Saturday mornings it fills with Naschmarkt shoppers. (05, Hamburgerstrasse 20; ⊘9am-2am; Ⓤ Kettenbrückengasse, Pilgramgasse)

Barfly's Club COCKTAIL BAR

13 🚇 Map p82, B3

This low-lit, sophisticated bar is famous for its 500-strong cocktail list (the menu is over 1cm thick) and intimate ambience, which attracts a regular crowd of journalists and actors. It's decorated with photos of Hemingway, Fidel Castro, Che Guevara, the Rat Pack and Marilyn Monroe. At around €14 a pop, drinks aren't cheap, but they're among the city's best. (www.castillo.at; 06, Esterhazygasse 33; ⊘8pm-2am Sun-Thu, to 4am Fri & Sat; Ⓤ Neubaugasse, Zieglergasse)

Café Jelinek COFFEE

14 🚇 Map p82, B4

With none of the polish or airs and graces of some other coffee houses, this

MUELLER, JOSEF/SHUTTERSTOCK ©

Musikverein

shabbily grand cafe is Viennese through and through. The wood-burning stove, picture-plastered walls and faded velvet armchairs draw people from all walks of life with their cocoon-like warmth. Join locals lingering over freshly roasted coffee, cake and the daily newspapers. (www.steman.at; 06, Otto-Bauer-Gasse 5; ⊘9am-9pm; Ⓤ Zieglergasse)

Club U   BAR, CLUB

15 Ⓡ Map p82, G2

Club U occupies one of Otto Wagner's Stadtbahn Pavillons (p85) on Karlsplatz. It's a small, student-favourite bar-club with regular DJs and a wonderful outdoor seating area overlooking the pavilions and park. (www.club-u. at; 04, Künstlerhauspassage; ⊘9pm-4am; Ⓤ Karlsplatz)

Wieden Bräu   MICROBREWERY

16 Ⓡ Map p82, F4

Helles, *Märzen* and *Radler* beers are brewed year-round at this upbeat microbrewery, and there are a few seasonal choices, including a ginger beer and hemp beer. All are brewed in keeping with the 1516 German Purity Law and are matched with Austrian classics such as schnitzel and goulash. Retreat to the garden in summer. (www.wieden-braeu.at; 04, Waaggasse 5; ⊘11.30am-midnight Sep-Jun,

4pm-midnight Sat & Sun Jul & Aug; 🛜;
Ⓤ Taubstummengasse)

Entertainment

Musikverein   CONCERT VENUE

17 ⭐ Map p82, H2

The opulent Musikverein holds the
proud title of the best acoustics of
any concert hall in Austria, which
the Vienna Philharmonic Orchestra
embraces. The lavish interior can
be visited by 45-minute guided tour
(in English and German; adult/child
€6.50/4) at 10am, 11am and noon
Monday to Saturday. Smaller-scale
performances are held in the Brahms
Saal. There are no student tickets.
(☎ 01-505 81 90; www.musikverein.at; 01,
Musikvereinsplatz 1; tickets €24-95, standing
room €4-6; ⊘ box office 9am-8pm Mon-Fri, to
1pm Sat Sep-Jun, 9am-noon Mon-Fri Jul & Aug;
Ⓤ Karlsplatz)

Burgtheater   THEATRE

18 ⭐ Map p82, F1

The Burgtheater hasn't lost its touch
over the years – this is one of the foremost theatres in the German-speaking
world, staging some 800 performances
a year, which reach from Shakespeare
to Woody Allen plays. The theatre also
runs the 500-seater Akademietheater,
which was built between 1911 and
1913. (National Theatre; ☎ 01-514 44 4440;
www.burgtheater.at; 01, Universitätsring 2;
seats €7.50-61, standing room €3.50, students

€9; ⊘ box office 9am-5pm Mon-Fri; 🚋 D, 1, 2
Rathaus, Ⓤ Rathaus)

Volksoper   OPERA, DANCE

19 ⭐ Map p82, F1

Offering a more intimate experience than the Staatsoper, the
Volksoper specialises in operettas,
dance performances, musicals and a
handful of standard, heavier operas.

Standing and impaired-view tickets go for between €3 to €10 and, like many venues, there is a plethora of discounts and reduced tickets for sale 30 minutes before performances. The Volksoper closes for July and August. (People's Opera; 📞01-514 44 3670; www.volksoper.at; 09, Währinger Strasse 78; ⏱Sep-Jun; Ⓤ Währinger Strasse)

Theater an der Wien
THEATRE

20 ⭐ Map p82, F2

The Theater an der Wien has hosted some monumental premiere performances, including Beethoven's *Fidelo,* Mozart's *Die Zauberflöte* and Strauss Jnr's *Die Fledermaus.* These days, besides staging musicals, dance and concerts, it's re-established its reputation for high-quality opera, with one premiere each month. Student tickets go on sale 30 minutes before shows; standing-room tickets are available one hour prior to performances. (📞01-588 85; www.theater-wien.at; 06, Linke Wienzeile 6; tickets €10-160, standing room €7, student tickets €10-15; ⏱box office 10am-6pm Mon-Sat, 2-6pm Sun; Ⓤ Karlsplatz)

Shopping

Blühendes Konfekt
FOOD

21 🔒 Map p82, A4

Violets, forest strawberries and cherry blossom, mint and oregano – Michael Diewald makes the most of what grows wild and in his garden to create confectionery that fizzes with seasonal flavour. Peek through to the workshop to see flowers and herbs being deftly transformed into one-of-a-kind bonbons and mini bouquets that are edible works of art. (www.bluehendes-konfekt.com; 06, Schmalzhofgasse 19; ⏱10am-6.30pm Wed-Fri; Ⓤ Zieglergasse, Westbahnhof)

Beer Lovers
DRINKS

22 🔒 Map p82, D3

A wonderland of craft beers, this emporium stocks over 1000 labels from over 125 different breweries in over 70 styles, with more being sourced every day. Tastings are offered regularly, and cold beers are available in the walk-in glass fridge and in refillable growlers. It also stocks craft ciders, small-batch liqueurs and boutique nonalcoholic drinks such as ginger beers. (http://beerlovers.at; 06, Gumpendorfer Strasse 35; ⏱11am-8pm Mon-Fri, 10am-5pm Sat; Ⓤ Kettenbrückengasse)

feinedinge
CERAMICS

23 🔒 Map p82, F4

Sandra Haischberger makes exquisite porcelain that reveals a clean modern aesthetic at her atelier shop. Her range of home accessories, tableware and lighting is minimalistic, but features sublime details, such as crockery in chalky pastels, filigree lamps that cast exquisite patterns and candle holders embellished with floral and butterfly motifs. (www.feinedinge.at; 05, Margaretenstrasse 35; ⏱10am-6pm Mon-Wed & Sat, to 7.30pm Thu & Fri; Ⓤ Kettenbrückengasse)

Gabarage Upcycling Design

DESIGN STORE

24 Map p82, F3

Recycled design, ecology and social responsibility underpin the quirky designs at Gabarage. Old bowling pins become vases, rubbish bins get a new life as tables and chairs, advertising tarpaulins morph into bags, and traffic lights are transformed into funky lights. (www.gabarage.at; 06, Schleifmühlgasse 6; ⏲10am-6pm Mon-Thu, 10am-7pm Fri, 11am-5pm Sat; Ⓤ Taubstummengasse)

Lichterloh

HOMEWARES

25 Map p82, E2

This massive, ultracool space is filled with iconic furniture from the 1900s to 1970s, by names such as Eames, Thonet and Mies Van Der Rohe. Even if you're not planning to lug home a sleek Danish sideboard, it's worth a look at this veritable gallery of modern furniture design. (www.lichterloh.com; 06, Gumpendorfer Strasse 15-17; ⏲11am-6.30pm Tue-Fri, 10am-2pm Sat; Ⓤ Museumsquartier)

Mein Design

FASHION & ACCESSORIES

26 Map p82, E4

Boutique owner and designer Ulrike gives young Austrian designers a platform for showcasing their fresh, innovative fashion and accessories at this boutique-workshop, where the accent is on quality and sustainability.

Local Life
Vienna's Naschmarkt

Vienna's aromatic **Naschmarkt** (Map p82, F2; 06, Linke & Rechte Wienzeile; ⏲6am-7.30pm Mon-Fri, to 6pm Sat; Ⓤ Karlsplatz, Kettenbrückengasse) unfurls over 500m along Linke Wienzeile between the U4 stops of Kettenbrückengasse and Karlsplatz. The western (Kettengasse) end has all sorts of meats, fruit and vegetables (including exotic varieties), spices, wines, cheeses, olives, Indian and Middle Eastern specialities and fabulous kebab and falafel stands. In all, there are 123 fixed stalls, including a slew of sit-down restaurants.

Another 35 places are allocated to temporary stalls such as farmers' stands. The market peters out at the eastern end to stalls selling Indian fabrics, jewellery and trashy trinkets. An adjoining **Flohmarkt** (Flea Market; Map p82, E3); 05, Linke Wienzeile; ⏲6.30am-6pm Sat; Ⓤ Kettenbrückengasse) sets up on Saturdays.

Displays change every few months; you might find anything from beautifully made children's clothes to jewellery fashioned from recycled tyres and silk blouses emblazoned with photographs of Vienna icons. (www.mein-design.org; 04, Kettenbrückengasse 6; ⏲11am-6pm Tue-Fri, 10am-3pm Sat; Ⓤ Kettenbrückengasse)

Explore

Schloss Belvedere to the Canal

The crowning glory of this art-rammed neighbourhood is Schloss Belvedere and its gardens, which can easily absorb an entire day of your time. Spread out across the neighbourhood, other crowd-pullers include some cracking cafes, delis and restaurants that make breaks between sightseeing all the more pleasurable.

The Sights in a Day

☀ **Schloss Belvedere** (p94) is overwhelming in both scale and substance, so it makes sense to start here, exploring its sumptuously frescoed baroque halls, replete with Klimt, Schiele and Kokoschka artworks.

☀ Break for lunch at nostalgic Café Goldegg before returning to the palace to wander its landscaped **gardens** (p97), which drop like the sudden fall of a theatre curtain to reveal Vienna's skyline; stop for a drink at microbrewery Salm Bräu. Absorbing museums in the area include the **Heeresgeschichtliches Museum** (p104), covering military history, and **Museum für Angewandte Kunst** (MAK; p104), showcasing applied arts.

☾ After dining on homemade cheeses and other delicacies at **Lingenhel** (p109), catch a diverse program of music at venues such as the **Konzerthaus** (p110).

For a local's day in Schloss Belvedere to the Canal, see p100.

◉ Top Sights
Schloss Belvedere (p94)

◯ Local Life
Green Escape (p100)

♥ Best of Vienna

Food
Meierei im Stadtpark (p106)

Steirereck im Stadtpark (p105)

Lingenhel (p109)

Drinking & Nightlife
Salm Bräu (p109)

Entertainment
Konzerthaus (p110)

Radiokulturhaus (p110)

Art
Schloss Belvedere (p94)

Getting There

Ⓤ **U-Bahn** Taubstummengasse and Südtiroler Platz stations, both on the U1 line, are close to Schloss Belvedere.

🚃 **Tram** Tram 2 trundles around the Ring (for MAK, Stadtpark), tram 1 to Radetzkyplatz (for the Hundertwasser sights), while trams 71 and D take you to Belvedere.

Top Sights
Schloss Belvedere

A masterpiece of total art, Belvedere is one of the world's finest baroque palaces. Designed by Johann Lukas von Hildebrandt (1668–1745), it was built as a summer residence for the brilliant military strategist Prince Eugene of Savoy, conqueror of the Turks in 1718. Eugene had grown up around the court of Louis XIV and it shows – this is a chateau to rival Versailles.

Map p102, B6

www.belvedere.at

adult/child Oberes Belvedere €14/free, Unteres Belvedere €12/free, combined ticket €20/free

🕙 10am-6pm

🚊 D, 71 Schwarzenbergplatz, Ⓤ Taubstummengasse, Südtiroler Platz

Oberes Belvedere

Rising splendidly above the gardens and commanding sweeping views of Vienna's skyline, the **Oberes Belvedere** (Upper Belvedere; 03, Prinz-Eugen-Strasse 27; adult/child €14/free; ☺10am-6pm) is one of Vienna's unmissable sights. Built between 1717 and 1723, its peerless art collection, showcased in rooms replete with marble, frescoes and stucco, attests to the unfathomable wealth and cultured tastes of the Habsburg Empire.

The **Sala Terrena** is a grand prelude to the ground floor, with four colossal Atlas pillars supporting the weight of its delicately stuccoed vault. Spread across four beautifully frescoed rooms, **Medieval Art** leads you through the artistic development of the age, with an exceptional portfolio of Gothic sculpture and altarpieces, many from Austrian abbeys and monasteries. Top billing goes to the Master of Grosslobming's sculptural group, whose fluid, expressive works embodied the figurative ideal; among them is the faceless *St George with Dragon* (1395), with a rather tame-looking dragon at his feet. Other heavenly treasures include Joachim's polyptych *Albrechtsaltar* (1435), one of the foremost examples of Gothic realism, and the *Znaim Altar* (1445), a gilded glorification of faith showing the Passion of Christ.

Modern Art & Interwar Period is particularly strong on Austrian expressionism. Attention-grabbers here include Oskar Kokoschka's richly animated portrait of art-nouveau painter *Carl Moll* (1913). Egon Schiele is represented by works both haunting and beguiling, such as *Death and the Maiden* (1915) and his portrait of six-year-old *Herbert Rainer* (1910). Other standouts include Oskar Laske's staggeringly detailed *Ship of Fools* (1923) and Max Oppenheimer's musical masterpiece *The Philharmonic* (1935), with a baton-swinging Gustav Mahler.

☑ **Top Tips**

▸ Order tickets online to save time and money.

▸ Combined ticket options are available, including one covering the Upper and Lower Belvedere and 21er Haus (adult/child €23/free).

▸ Visit the website for details on guided tours and upcoming exhibitions.

▸ Dodge the crowds by arriving just before the palace opens – queues are at their worst at peak summer times.

✗ **Take a Break**

Take a 10-minute stroll to Café Goldegg (p105) for a light lunch and a blast of Viennese nostalgia.

Quaff a cold one post-palace tour at Salm Bräu (p109) microbrewery.

The 1st-floor **Vienna 1880–1914** collection is a holy grail for Klimt fans, with an entire room devoted to erotic golden wonders such as *Judith* (1901), *Salome* (1909), *Adam and Eve* (1917) and *The Kiss* (1908). Works by German symbolist painter Max Klinger (1857–1920), as well as portraits by Secessionist Koloman Moser and Norwegian expressionist Edvard Munch, also feature. The centrepiece is the **Marmorsaal**, a chandelier-lit marble, stucco and trompe l'oeil confection, crowned by Carlo Innocenzo Carlone's ceiling fresco (1721–23) celebrating the glorification of Prince Eugène. **Baroque & Early-19th-Century Art** pays tribute to Austrian masters of the age, endowed with highlights such

as Johann Michael Rottmayr's lucid *Susanna and the Elders* (1692) and Paul Troger's chiaroscuro *Christ on the Mount of Olives* (1750).

In **Neoclassicism, Romanticism & Biedermeier Art**, you'll find outstanding works such as Georg Waldmüller's *Corpus Christi Morning* (1857), a joyous snapshot of impish lads and flower girls bathed in honeyed light. Representative of the neoclassical period are clearer, more emotionally restrained pieces such as Jacques-Louis David's gallant *Napoleon on Great St Bernard Pass* (1801) and François Gérard's portrait *Count Moritz Christian Fries and Family* (1804). The romantic period is headlined by the wistful, brooding landscapes and seascapes of

SCHLOSS BELVEDERE & GARDENS

19th-century German painter Caspar David Friedrich.

French masters share the limelight with their Austrian and German contemporaries in **Realism & Impressionism**, where you'll feel the artistic pull of Renoir's softly evocative *Woman after the Bath* (1876), Monet's sun-dappled *Garden at Giverny* (1902) and Van Gogh's *Plain at Auvers* (1890), where wheat fields ripple under a billowing sky. Lovis Corinth's tranquil *Woman Reading Near a Goldfish Tank* (1911) and Max Liebermann's *Hunter in the Dunes* (1913) epitomise the German Impressionist style.

Gardens

Belvedere means 'beautiful view'. The reason for this name becomes apparent in the baroque **garden** (03, Rennweg/Prinz-Eugen-Strasse; ⏱6.30am-8pm, shorter hours in winter; 🚇D) linking the upper and lower palace, which was laid out around 1700 in classical French style by Dominique Girard, a pupil of André le Nôtre of Versailles fame. Set along a **central axis**, the gently sloping garden commands a broad view of Vienna's skyline, with the Stephansdom and the Hofburg punctuating the horizon.

The three-tiered garden is lined by clipped box hedges and flanked by ornamental parterres. As you stroll to the **Lower Cascade**, with its frolicking water nymphs, look out for Greco-Roman statues of the eight muses and cherubic putti embodying the 12 months of the year. Mythical beasts squirt water across the **Upper Cascade**, which spills down five steps into the basin below. Guarding the approach to the Oberes Belvedere are winged sphinxes, symbols of power and wisdom, which look as though they are about to take flight any minute.

South of the Oberes Belvedere is the **Alpengarten** (www.bundesgaerten.at; 03, Prinz-Eugen-Strasse 27; adult/child €3.50/2.50; ⏲10am-6pm late Mar-early Aug; 🚇D, O, 18), a Japanese-style garden nurturing Alpine species, at its fragrant best from spring to summer, when clematis,

Understand
Adele Bloch-Bauer

The Nazis seized the property of the wealthy Jewish Bloch-Bauer family following the 1938 *Anschluss*. Among their substantial collection were five Klimt originals, including the *Portrait of Adele Bloch-Bauer I* (1907). The stolen paintings hung in the Oberes Belvedere until 2006, when a US Supreme Court ruled the Austrian government must return the paintings to their rightful owner, Adele Bloch-Bauer's niece and heir Maria Altmann. The portrait alone fetched US$135 million at auction, at the time the highest price ever paid for a painting, and today hangs in the New York Neue Galerie.

rhododendrons, roses and peonies are in bloom. North from here is the larger Botanischer Garten (p101), belonging to the Vienna University, with tropical glasshouses and 11,500 botanical species, including Chinese dwarf bamboo and Japanese plum yews.

Unteres Belvedere

Built between 1712 and 1716, **Unteres Belvedere** (Lower Belvedere; 03, Rennweg 6; adult/child €12/free; ⏲10am-6pm Thu-Tue, to 9pm Wed; 🚇D) is a baroque feast of state apartments and ceremonial rooms. Most lavish of all is the red marble **Marmorsaal**, an ode to Prince Eugène's military victories, with stucco trophies, medallions and Martino Altomonte's ceiling fresco showing the glorification of the prince and Apollo surrounded by muses. At eye level are sculptures taken from Georg Raphael Donner's mid-18th-century **fountain** on Neuer Markt. Snake-bearing Providentia (Prudence) rises above four putti grappling with fish, each of which symbolises a tributary of the Danube.

In the **Groteskensaal**, foliage intertwines with fruit, birds and mythological beasts in the fanciful grotesque style that was all the rage in baroque times. This leads through to the **Marmorgalerie**, a vision of frilly white stucco and marble, encrusted with cherubs and war trophies. The niches originally displayed three classical statues from Herculaneum (now in Dresden), which inspired baroque sculptor Domenico Paroditom to create the neoclassical statues you see today. Maria Theresia put her stamp on the

palace in the adjacent **Goldkabinett**, a mirrored cabinet dripping in gold.

Temporary exhibitions are held in the **Orangery**, with a walkway gazing grandly over Prince Eugène's private garden. Attached to the Orangery is the **Prunkstall**, the former royal stables, where you can trot through a 150-piece collection of Austrian medieval art, including religious scenes, altarpieces, and Gothic triptychs.

Combined Tickets

Ordering printable tickets online saves time, but they can't be exchanged or refunded. Several money-saving combined ticket options are available, including one covering the Upper Belvedere, Lower Belvedere and 21er Haus (adult/under 19 years €23/free) and another covering the Upper and Lower Belvedere (adult/under 19 years €20/free). Combined tickets are valid for two weeks after the first visit.

Guided Tours

Audio guides can be hired for €4 and are available in German, English, French, Italian, Spanish, Japanese and Russian; you'll need to leave ID as a deposit. One-hour themed tours on a specific period or artist cost €4 and are in German. Times and themes vary (see the online calendar), but generally there are tours at 3pm and/or 4pm on weekends, plus 10.30am on Sunday.

Local Life
Green Escape

Get a breath of fresh air on this stroll, which starts at a farmers market, stops off for coffee and passes some of Vienna's most adventurous architecture before bringing you down to the parkland-lined Danube Canal. More parks along this green route include the Stadtpark (city park) and beautiful botanic gardens.

....

❶ Market Shop

The stalls are piled high with olives, flowers, farm-fresh meat and cheese at the **Rochusmarkt** (03, Landstrasser Hauptstrasse; ◷6am-7.30pm Mon-Fri, to 5pm Sat; ⓤRochusgasse). There are a handful of cafes, takeaway joints and bakeries on the square.

❷ Coffee Stop

A withered beauty of a coffee house, **Café Zartl** (03, Rasumofskygasse 7;

⊘7am-11pm; 📶; 🚋1 Rasumofskygasse, Ⓤ Rochusgasse) pings you back to when it opened in 1883, with its striped banquettes, cocoon-like warmth and, at times, somnambulant staff. Come for lazy breakfasts, people-watching and coffee with delightfully flaky strudel. You'll be mostly among regulars.

❸ Radical Architecture

Residential apartment block the **Hundertwasserhaus** (03, cnr Löwengasse & Kegelgasse; 🚋1 Hetzgasse) bears all the wackily creative hallmarks of Vienna's radical architect Hundertwasser with its curvy lines, crayon-bright colours and mosaics. Across the road, cafe- and shop-filled Kalke Village is also the handiwork of Hundertwasser, created from an old Michelin factory. In typical Hundertwasser fashion, it has colourful ceramics and a distinct absence of straight lines.

❹ Beach Bar

You'd swear you're by the sea at hopping canalside **Strandbar Herrmann** (www.strandbarherrmann.at; 03, Herrmannpark; ⊘10am-2am Apr-early Oct; 📶; 🚌O Hintere Zollamstrasse, Ⓤ Schwedenplatz), with beach chairs, sand, DJ beats and hordes of Viennese livin' it up on summer evenings. Cocktails are two for the price of one during happy hour (6pm to 7pm). Cool trivia: it's located on Herrmannpark, named after picture postcard inventor Emanuel Herrmann (1839–1902).

❺ Park Life

Opened in 1862, the **Stadtpark** (City Park; 01, 03; admission free; 🚋2 Weihburggasse, Ⓤ Stadtpark) is a tranquil pocket of greenery, with winding paths and willow tree–rimmed duck ponds. It's great for strolling or relaxing in the sun and a favourite lunchtime escape for Innere Stadt workers. The park spans the Wien River, which empties into the Danube Canal.

❻ Hidden Cafe

Look for the house number, not the name, as there's no sign at **Café am Heumarkt** (03, Am Heumarkt 15; ⊘9am-11pm Mon-Fri; Ⓤ Stadtpark), an old-school charmer of a coffee house. Inside, it's a 1950s time-warp – all shiny parquet, leather banquettes and marble tables. Do as the locals do: grab a newspaper, play billiards and unwind over coffee and no-nonsense Viennese grub.

❼ Botanic Gardens

The **Botanischer Garten** (www.botanik. univie.ac.at; 03, Rennweg 14; admission free; ⊘10am-1hr before dusk; 🚋71, O), belonging to the Vienna University, have tropical glasshouses and 11,500 species from six continents, including botanical wonders like Chinese dwarf bamboo, gingko biloba, tulip trees and Japanese plum yews.

For reviews see

◉ Top Sights — p94
◉ Sights — p104
✖ Eating — p105
◐ Drinking — p109
◒ Entertainment — p110

Sights

Heeresgeschichtliches Museum
MUSEUM

1 ◉ Map p102, C8

The superb Heeresgeschichtliches Museum is housed in the Arsenal, a large neo-Byzantine barracks and munitions depot. Spread over two floors, the museum works its way from the Thirty Years' War (1618–48) to WWII, taking in the Hungarian Uprising and the Austro-Prussian War (ending in 1866), the Napoleonic and Turkish Wars, and WWI. Highlights on the 1st floor include the Great Seal of Mustafa Pasha, which fell to Prince Eugene of Savoy in the Battle of Zenta in 1697. (Museum of Military History; www. hgm.or.at; 03, Arsenal; adult/under 19yr €6/free, 1st Sun of month free; ☺9am-5pm; Ⓤ Südtiroler Platz)

Museum für Angewandte Kunst
MUSEUM

2 ◉ Map p102, B2

MAK is devoted to craftsmanship and art forms in everyday life. Each exhibition room showcases a different style, which includes Renaissance, baroque, orientalism, historicism, empire, art deco and the distinctive metalwork of the Wiener Werkstätte. Contemporary artists were invited to present the rooms in ways they felt were appropriate, resulting in eye-catching and unique displays. The 20th-century design and architecture room is one of the most fascinating, and Frank Gehry's cardboard chair is a gem. (MAK, Museum of Applied Arts; www.mak. at; 01, Stubenring 5; adult/under 19yr €9.90/free, 6-10pm Tue free, tours €2; ☺10am-6pm Wed-Sun, to 10pm Tue, English tours noon Sun; 🚋2 Stubentor, Ⓤ Stubentor)

KunstHausWien
MUSEUM

3 ◉ Map p102, E1

The KunstHausWien, with its bulging ceramics, wonky surfaces, checkerboard facade, Technicolour mosaic tilework and rooftop sprouting plants and trees, bears the inimitable hallmark of eccentric Viennese artist and ecowarrior Hundertwasser (1928–2000), who famously called the straight line 'godless'. It is an ode to his playful, boldly creative work, as well as to his green politics. (Art House Vienna; www.kunsthauswien.com; 03, Untere Weissgerberstrasse 13; adult/child €11/5; ☺10am-6pm; 🚋1, Ⓞ Radetzkyplatz)

Fälschermuseum
MUSEUM

4 ◉ Map p102, E2

Wow, a museum with Schiele, Raphael, Rembrandt and Marc Chagall paintings that nobody knows about? Well, that's because they are all fakes, though spotting the difference is a near impossibility for the untrained eye. The tiny, privately run Fälschermuseum opens a fascinating window on the world of art forgeries. Besides giving background on the who, how, when and what, the museum recounts some incredible

KunstHausWien

stories about master forgers who briefly managed to pull the wool over the experts' eyes. (Museum of Art Fakes; www.faelschermuseum.com; 03, Löwengasse 28; adult/child €5.50/3; ☉10am-5pm Tue-Sun; 🚋1 Hetzgasse)

Eating

Steirereck im Stadtpark

GASTRONOMY €€€

5 🍴 Map p102, B3

Heinz Reitbauer is at the culinary helm of this two-starred Michelin restaurant, beautifully lodged in a 20th-century former dairy building in the leafy Stadtpark. His tasting menus are an exuberant feast, fizzing with natural, integral flavours that speak of a chef with exacting standards. Wine pairing is an additional €79/89 (six/seven courses). (📞01-713 31 68; http://steirereck.at; 03, Am Heumarkt 2a; mains €48-52, 6-/7-course menus €142/152; ☉11.30am-2.30pm & 6.30pm-midnight Mon-Fri; 🚇Stadtpark)

Café Goldegg

CAFÉ €

6 🍴 Map p102, A8

Goldegg is a coffee house in the classic Viennese mould, with its green velvet booths, wood panelling, billiard tables and art-nouveau sheen – but with a twist. Staff are refreshingly attentive, and alongside menu stalwarts such as goulash, you'll find lighter dishes like toasted paninis with homemade basil pesto and Ayurvedic vegetable curries. (www.cafegoldegg.at; 04, Argentinierstrasse 49; snacks €3.50-6, mains €10-13; ⏰8am-8pm Mon-Fri, 9am-8pm Sat, 9am-7pm Sun; 🛜🖊; Ⓤ Südtiroler Platz)

Meierei im Stadtpark AUSTRIAN €€

In the green surrounds of Stadtpark, the Meierei (see 5 ✕ Map p102, B3) is most famous for its goulash served with lemon, capers and creamy dumplings (€18) and its selection of 120 types of cheese. Served until noon, the bountiful breakfast features gastronomic showstoppers such as poached duck egg with sweet potato, cress and wild mushrooms, and warm curd-cheese strudel with elderberry compote. (🖉01-713 31 68; http://steirereck.

Local Life
Zentralfriedhof

When a Wiener says, '*Er hat den 71er genommen*' ('He took the No 71'), they are, metaphorically speaking, referring to the end of the line: **Zentralfriedhof** (www.friedhoefewien.at; 11, Simmeringer Hauptstrasse 232-244; ⏰7am-8pm, shorter hours in winter; 🚋6, 71 Zentralfriedhof). The cemetery's mammoth scale (2.4 sq km, more than three million 'residents') has made its tram line a euphemism for death. With leafy avenues and overgrown monuments, it's a calming place to wander.

at; 03, Am Heumarkt 2a; set breakfasts €20-24, mains €11.50-22; ⏰8am-11pm Mon-Fri, 9am-7pm Sat & Sun; 🖊; Ⓤ Stadtpark)

Joseph Brot BISTRO €€

7 ✕ Map p102, C3

Purveyors of some of Vienna's finest bread, Joseph Brot's newest bakery, bistro and patisserie is a winner. Besides wonderfully fresh loaves – organic olive-tomato ciabatta and rye-honey-lavender, for instance – it does wholesome breakfasts, speciality teas, healthy smoothies and utterly divine pastries. Season-driven specials such as sea bream with tomatoes, artichokes and olives star on the lunch menu in the stripped-back bistro. (03, Landstrasser Hauptstrasse 4; breakfast €6.70-14.60, lunch mains €12.50-17.50; ⏰bakery 7.30am-9pm Mon-Fri, 8am-6pm Sat & Sun, bistro 8am-9pm Mon-Fri & 8am-6pm Sat & Sun; Ⓤ Wien Mitte)

Cafe Menta CAFE €

8 ✕ Map p102, D1

Cafe Menta cuts a nouveau-retro look, with its mint-green walls, bright, wood-floored interior and contemporary bistro seating. Mezze-style sharing plates are the way to go for a taste of mini dishes such as sea-bass kebabs and aubergine halloumi rolls. It also rustles up tasty salads, soups, pasta and ciabattas (including some vegan options) and a cooling homemade mint ice tea. (🖉01-966 84 23; www.cafementa.at; 03; Radetzkyplatz 4; lunch €7.50, tasting platter €13, mains €7.50-15.50; ⏰8.30am-midnight)

Understand

Klimt in Vienna

The works of Gustav Klimt (1862–1918) – the shining star of Austria's Jugendstil (Art Nouveau) age – are as resonant today as they were when he scandalised the rigid artistic establishment in fin de siècle Vienna with his exotic, erotic style. Schloss Belvedere (p94) contains the world's largest Klimt collection.

Klimt & the Female Form

Klimt's fascination with women is a common thread in his paintings. The artist was most at ease in women's company and lived with his mother and two sisters even at the height of his career. Despite his long-term relationship with fashion designer Emilie Flöge, Klimt had countless affairs with his models and fathered around 14 illegitimate children. Though of humble origins, Klimt was quickly sought out by high-society ladies wishing to have their portrait done.

The Kiss (1908; Oberes Belvedere)

A couple draped in elaborate robes are shown entwined in an embrace in a flowered meadow. Rumours suggest this to be Klimt and his lifelong lover, Emilie Flöge. With a sinuous waterfall of gold-leaf and elaborate patterning set against a stardust backdrop, the couple appear to transgress the canvas.

Adam & Eve (1918; Oberes Belvedere)

Klimt was working on this biblical wonder when he suddenly died of a stroke on 6 February 1918. Adam is less prominent in the background, while in the foreground stands Eve, a celestial vision of radiant skin, a cascade of golden hair, with anemones scattered at her feet.

Judith (1901; Oberes Belvedere)

One of Klimt's seminal art works, this is an entrancing evocation of the Old Testament heroine Judith, a rich widow who charms and decapitates Holofernes (look for his severed head in the right-hand corner of the canvas). The use of gold leaf and mosaic-like detail is typical of Klimt's golden period, which was inspired by the Byzantine imagery he saw on his travels to Venice.

Salm Bräu

Gasthaus Wild

AUSTRIAN €€

9 🍴 Map p102, D1

Gasthaus Wild, formerly a dive of a *Beisl,* has in recent years morphed into a great *neo-Beisl.* Its dark, wood-panelled interior retains a traditional look, and the menu includes flavour-some favourites such as goulash, schnitzel with potato salad, and papri-ka chicken with *Spätzle* (egg noodles). The menu changes regularly, the vibe is relaxed, the staff welcoming and the wine selection good. (📞01-920 94 77; http://gasthaus-wild.at; 03, Radetzkyplatz 1; 2-course lunch menus €8.30-10.30, mains €11-27.50; ⏱9am-1am Mon-Fri, to midnight Sun; 🖊; 🚋1, 🚆 Radetzkyplatz)

Gmoakeller

AUSTRIAN €€

10 🍴 Map p102, B4

Sizzling and stirring since 1858, this atmospheric cellar is as traditional as it gets, with parquet floors, brick vaults and warm wood-panelling. The classic grub – *Zwiebelrost-braten* (onion-topped roast beef) or Carinthian *Kas'nudeln* (cheese noodles) – goes nicely with tangy Austrian wines. Tables spill out onto the pavement in summer. (📞01-712 53 10; www.gmoakeller.at; 03; Am Heumarkt 25; mains €9-18; ⏱11am-midnight Mon-Sat; 🚇Stadtpark)

Hidden Kitchen Park

DELI €

11 ⊗ Map p102, C3

Fresh, healthy food takes centre stage at the modern, buzzy Hidden Kitchen Park. The emphasis is on top-quality produce in creative salads such as lemon-herb couscous and rocket with antipasti and polenta crumble, wholesome stews and soups. (www.hiddenkitchen.at; 03, Invalidenstrasse 19; main, salad & soup €10; ⊘8am-5pm Mon-Fri, 10am-4pm Sat; Ⓤ Wien Mitte)

Salon Plafond

AUSTRIAN €€

Located in the MAK, Salon Plafond (see 2 ◉ Map p102, B2) is the gallery's latest venture, with an ingredient-focused menu that plays up careful sourcing. The menu seesaws with the seasons, with starters such as autumn salad with pomegranate and walnut piquing the appetite for mains such as venison with Jerusalem artichoke. (☏01-226 00 46; http://salonplafond.wien/de; 01, Stubenring 5; lunch mains €9-12, dinner mains €18-27; ⊘10am-midnight; 🖢; 🚋2 Stubentor, Ⓤ Stubentor)

Drinking

Salm Bräu

MICROBREWERY

12 🍺 Map p102, B6

Salm Bräu brews its own *Helles*, *Pils* (pilsner), *Märzen* (red-coloured beer with a strong malt taste), *G'mischt* (half *Helles* and half *Dunkel* – dark) and *Weizen* (full-bodied wheat beer,

slightly sweet in taste). It is smack next to Schloss Belvedere and hugely popular, with a happy hour from 3pm to 5pm Monday to Friday and noon to 4pm Saturday. (www.salmbraeu.com; 03, Rennweg 8; ⊘11am-midnight; 🚋71 Unteres Belvedere, Ⓤ Karlsplatz)

Urania

BAR

13 🍷 Map p102, C1

Another addition to the canal's ever-increasing stock of bars, Urania occupies the 1st floor of a rejuvenated cinema and observatory complex. Its slick, clean decor, elevated position overlooking the canal and extensive cocktail selection are all big pluses. (www.barurania.com; 01, Uraniastrasse 1;

Ⓠ Local Life

Lingenhel

Lodged in a 200-year-old house, multi-purpose **Lingenhel** (Map p102, E4; ☏01-710 15 66; www.lingenhel.com; 03; Landstrasser Hauptstrasse 74; mains €19-24; ⊘shop 8am-8pm, restaurant 8am-10pm Mon-Sat; Ⓤ Rochusgasse) sells salamis, wines and own-dairy cheeses in its shop (cheese-making courses available), while chef Daniel Hoffmeister helms the kitchen in the pared-back, whitewashed restaurant. Simple, season-inflected food might include char with kohlrabi and pork belly with aubergines. The bar is a stylish spot for a house vermouth and tonic.

⊙9am-midnight Mon-Fri, 2pm-midnight Sat, 9am-6pm Sun; 🚇2 Julius-Raab-Platz, Ⓤ Schwedenplatz)

Entertainment

Konzerthaus

CONCERT VENUE

14 ⭐ Map p102, B4

The Konzerthaus is a major venue in classical-music circles, but throughout the year ethnic music, rock, pop or jazz can also be heard in its hallowed halls. Up to three simultaneous performances, in the Grosser Saal, the Mozart Saal and the Schubert Saal,

---

🔍 Local Life
Schanigärten

When the weather warms up, life spills outdoors to the *Schanigärten*. Unlike *Gastgärten* (beer gardens), *Schanigärten* set up on public property such as pavements and sometimes parking areas and squares according to inexpensive permits issued by authorities, which are valid from 1 March to 15 November. Actual opening dates depend on the weather each season.

Beach bars pop up along the waterfront in summer, and are a great alternative for Viennese who don't join their fellow citizens decamping from the city during the July/August *Sommerpause* (summer break), when many of the city's restaurants, bars and smaller shops shut down.

---

can be staged; this massive complex also features another four concert halls. (☎01-242 002; www.konzerthaus. at; 03, Lothringerstrasse 20; ⊙box office 9am-7.45pm Mon-Fri, to 1pm Sat, plus 45min before performance; 🚇D Gusshausstrasse, Ⓤ Stadtpark)

Radiokulturhaus

CONCERT VENUE

15 ⭐ Map p102, A6

Expect anything from odes to Sinatra and R.E.M. or an evening dedicated to Beethoven and Mozart at the Radiokulturhaus. Housed in several performance venues including the Grosser Sendesaal – home to the Vienna Radio Symphony Orchestra and the Klangtheater (used primarily for radio plays) – this is one of Vienna's cultural hot spots. (☎01-501 70 377; http://radiokulturhaus.orf.at; 04, Argentinierstrasse 30a; tickets €7-27; ⊙box office 4-7pm Mon-Fri; 🚇D Plösslgasse, Ⓤ Taubstummengasse)

Arnold Schönberg Center

CLASSICAL MUSIC

16 ⭐ Map p102, B5

This brilliant repository of Arnold Schönberg's archival legacy is a cultural centre and celebration of the Viennese school of the early 20th century honouring the Viennese-born composer, painter, teacher, theoretician and innovator known for his 12-tone technique. The exhibition hall hosts intimate classical concerts, which in-the-know Wiener flock to. (☎01-712 18 88; www.schoenberg.at; 03, Schwarzenbergplatz 6,

Understand

Green Government

Vienna is a city-state, meaning the mayor doubles as the head of a state government. The capital has been governed by the Sozialdemokratischen Partei Österreichs (Social Democratic Party of Austria; SPÖ) and headed by an SPÖ mayor uninterrupted since 1945.

Under Bürgermeister (mayor) Dr Michael Häupl, the SPÖ governs Vienna in coalition with the Greens party, which picked up 10% of the 2015 vote. The next state elections will be held in 2020.

The goal of Vienna's ruling SPÖ party is to ensure the optimal quality of life by minimising resource consumption. Strategies include an 80% reduction of CO_2 emissions from 1990 levels (down from 3.1 tonnes per capita to 1 tonne), and for 50% of Vienna's gross energy consumption to originate from renewable sources such as solar and wind-turbine power. The target date for both is 2050, by which date diesel and petrol cars will be banned; a 15% reduction of motorised traffic is planned by 2030. Green spaces are planned to remain at over 50% of urban space within the city.

entrance at Zaunergasse 1; ⊗10am-5pm Mon-Fri; 🚊D Schwarzenbergplatz, Ⓤ Stadtpark)

Kursalon   CLASSICAL MUSIC

17 ⭐ Map p102, B3

Fans of Strauss and Mozart will love the performances at Kursalon, which holds daily evening concerts at 8.15pm devoted to the two masters of music in a splendid, refurbished Renaissance building. Also popular is the concert and dinner package (three- or four-course meal (not including drinks) at 6pm, followed by the concert) in the equally palatial

on-site restaurant. (☎01-512 57 90; www.kursalonwien.at; 01, Johannesgasse 33; tickets €42-95, concert with 3-course dinner €74-127, with 4-course dinner €79-132; 🚊2 Weihburggasse, Ⓤ Stadtpark)

Akademietheater   THEATRE

18 ⭐ Map p102, B4

Opened in 1922, the 500-seater Akademietheater is the second venue of Vienna's highly esteemed Burgtheater. It stages predominantly contemporary productions. (☎01-514 44 41 40; www.burgtheater.at; 03, Lisztstrasse 1; tickets €7-61; 🚊4A, Ⓤ Stadtpark)

Top Sights
Prater

Getting There

Ⓤ Praterstern (U1 and U2) is the main public transport link.

🚋 No 1 is a useful link between the southern portions of the Prater and the Ringstrasse.

The Prater (www.wiener-prater.at) describes two distinct areas of parkland, which together comprise the city's favourite outdoor playground. First up, as you enter, is the Würstelprater, with all the roller-coaster-looping, dodgem-bashing fun of the fair, where the iconic Riesenrad turns. The Unterer Prater is a vast swath of woodland park, where Habsburgs once went hunting. Today, it is perfect for gentle bike rides, walks and warm-day picnics.

Würstelprater

No matter how old you are, you're forever 10 years old with money burning a hole in your pocket at the **Würstelprater** (rides €1.50-5). Come summer, this funfair throngs with excitable tots and big kids, gorging on doughnuts and lugging around hoopla-won teddies. The fairground's 250 attractions reach from old-school ghost trains and merry-go-rounds to g-force, human cannon-like rides.

Several recent white-knuckle additions to the funfair have cranked up the fear factor, including the **Turbo Boost** that spins at 100km/h, the **Ejection Seat**, a ball that dangles daredevils 90m above the ground, and the **Space Shot**, which shoots thrill-seekers like bullets at up to 80km/h. The 4km **Liliputbahn** (mini railway) trundles between the Würstelprater and the Ernst-Happel-Stadion.

Riesenrad

Top of every Volksprater wish list is the **Riesenrad** (www.wienerriesenrad.com; 02, Prater 90; adult/child €9.50/4; ⏰9am-11.45pm, shorter hours in winter; ⓤPraterstern); at least for anyone of an age to recall Orson Welles' cuckoo clock speech in British film noir *The Third Man* (1949), set in a shadowy postwar Vienna. This icon also achieved celluloid fame in the James Bond flick *The Living Daylights* and *Before Sunrise,* directed by Richard Linklater.

Built in 1897 by Englishman Walter B Basset to celebrate the Golden Jubilee of Emperor Franz Josef I, the Ferris wheel rises to 65m and takes about 20 minutes to rotate its 430-tonne weight one complete circle – giving you ample time to snap some fantastic shots of the city spread out at your feet. It survived bombing in 1945 and has had dramatic lighting and a cafe at its base.

☑ **Top Tip**

▶ For a truly Viennese experience, visit the farmers market at **Karmelitermarkt** (02, Karmelitermarkt; ⏰6am-7.30pm Mon-Fri, to 5pm Sat; ⓡ2 Karmeliterplatz, ⓤTaborstrasse), before brunch at one of the deli-cafes.

✖ **Take a Break**

Housed in an 1898 mansion, retro-grand cafe **Supersense** (02, Praterstrasse 70; lunch special €5.50-6.50, breakfast €3.80-8; ⏰9am-7pm Mon-Fri, 10am-5pm Sat) has locally roasted coffee, breakfasts and daily specials.

Intimate bistro **Tempel** (☎01-214 01 79; www.restaurant-tempel.at; 02, Praterstrasse 56; mains €15.50-26, 2-/3-course lunch €14.50/18; ⏰noon-3pm & 6pm-midnight Tue-Fri, 6pm-midnight Sat; ⓤNestroyplatz) hides in a courtyard just off Praterstrasse.

Planetarium

The **Planetarium** (www.planetarium-wien.at; 02, Oswald-Thomas-Platz 1; adult/child €9/6.50; ☺show times vary; Ⓤ Praterstern), Vienna's extraterrestrial and interstellar viewfinder, is located on the edge of the Würstelprater behind the Riesenrad. Shows change on a regular basis, but usually focus on how the Earth fits into the cosmological scheme of things. Shows are in German.

Pratermuseum

Sharing the same building as the Planetarium, this **municipal museum** (www.wienmuseum.at; 02, Oswald-Thomas-Platz 1; adult/under 19yr €5/free; ☺10am-1pm & 2-6pm Tue-Sun Mar-Oct, 10am-1pm & 2-6pm Fri-Sun Nov-Feb; Ⓤ Praterstern) traces the history of the Würstelprater and its woodland neighbour. For all the life and splendour the Prater has seen, unfortunately its museum has only a rather dull mix of photos and stories, mainly from the 19th century. The antique slot machines, some of which are still functioning, are the museum's saving grace.

Unterer Prater

Few places in Vienna can match the Unterer Prater for fresh air, exercise and a burst of seasonal colour. Spread across 60 sq km, central Vienna's biggest park comprises woodlands of poplar and chestnut, meadows and tree-lined boulevards, as well as children's playgrounds, a swimming pool, golf course and racetrack.

Fringed by statuesque chestnut trees that are ablaze with russet and gold in autumn and billowing with delicate white blossom in late spring, the **Hauptallee** avenue is the Unterer Prater's central 4.5km vein, running as straight as a die from the Praterstern to the **Lusthaus** (☏01-728 95 65; 02, Freudenau 254; mains €11-19; ☺noon-10pm Mon-Fri, to 6pm Sat & Sun, shorter hours winter; ☎; ☒77A). Originally erected as a 16th-century hunting lodge, the Lusthaus pavilion was rebuilt in 1783 to host imperial festivities and the like. Today, it shelters a chandelier-lit cafe and restaurant.

Nearby: Augarten

The landscaped park **Augarten** (www.kultur.park.augarten.org; 03, Obere Augartenstrasse; ☺6am-dusk; Ⓤ Taborstrasse) dates from 1775 and is dotted with open meadows and criss-crossed by tree-lined paths. You can kick a ball in one section, let the kids stage a riot in a playground in another, or visit the porcelain museum **Porzellanmuseum im Augarten** (Augarten Porcelain Museum; www.augarten.at; 02, Obere Augartenstrasse 1; adult/child €7/5, incl guided tour €11/9; ☺10am-6pm Mon-Sat; Ⓤ Taborstrasse). Among the park's most eye-catching features are the austere Flaktürme (flak towers) in its northern and western corners.

Understand
The Third Man

Sir Alexander Korda asked English author Graham Greene to write a film about the four-power occupation of postwar Vienna. Greene flew to Vienna in 1948 and searched for inspiration with increasing desperation. Nothing came to mind until, with his departure imminent, Greene had lunch with a British intelligence officer who told him about the underground police who patrolled the huge network of sewers beneath the city, and the black-market trade in penicillin. Greene put the two ideas together and created his story.

Shot in Vienna in the same year, the film perfectly captures the atmosphere of postwar Vienna using an excellent play of shadow and light. The plot is simple but gripping: Holly Martins, an out-of-work writer played by Joseph Cotton, travels to Vienna at the request of his old schoolmate Harry Lime (played superbly by Orson Welles), only to find him dead under mysterious circumstances. Doubts over the death drag Martins into the black-market penicillin racket and the path of the multinational forces controlling Vienna. Accompanying the first-rate script, camera work and acting is a mesmerising soundtrack. After filming one night, director Carol Reed was dining at a *Heuriger* (wine tavern) and fell under the spell of Anton Karas' zither playing. Although Karas could neither read nor write music, Reed flew him to London to record the soundtrack. His bouncing, staggering 'Harry Lime Theme' dominated the film, became a chart hit and earned Karas a fortune.

The Third Man was an instant success. It won first prize at Cannes in 1949 and the Academy Award for Best Camera for a Black and White Movie in 1950, and was selected by the British Film Institute as 'favourite British film of the 20th century' in 1999. For years, the **Burg Kino** (☎01-587 84 06; www.burgkino.at; 01, Opernring 19; tickets €8-9.50; 🚊D, 1, 2 Burgring, ⓤMuseumsquartier) has screened the film on a weekly basis.

The film's popularity has spawned the **Third Man Private Collection** (www.3mpc.net; 04, Pressgasse 25; adult/child €8/4.50, guided tour incl musuem admission €10; ⏱2-6pm Sat, guided tours 2pm Wed; ⓤKettenbrückengasse). True aficionados may want to take the English-language **Third Man Tour** (☎01-774 89 01; www.viennawalks.com) of filming locations.

Top Sights
Schloss Schönbrunn

Getting There

U **U-Bahn** Schönbrunn is well connected to central Vienna by U-Bahn's green U4 line to either Schönbrunn and Hietzing.

🚊 **Tram** It's an easy tram ride on the 58 from Westbahnhof.

The Habsburg Empire is revealed in all its frescoed, gilded, chandelier-lit glory in the wondrously ornate apartments of Schloss Schönbrunn, which are among Europe's best-preserved baroque interiors. Stories about the first public performance of wunderkind Mozart or Empress Elisabeth's extreme beauty and fitness regimes bring Austrian history to life as you wander the 40 rooms open to the public.

State Apartments

The frescoed **Blue Staircase** makes a regal ascent to the palace's upper level. First up are the 19th-century apartments of Emperor Franz Josef I and his beloved wife Elisabeth. The tour whisks you through lavishly stuccoed, chandelier-lit apartments such as the **Billiard Room**, where army officials would pot balls while waiting to attend an audience, and Franz Josef's **study**, where he worked tirelessly from 5am. The iron bedstead and washstand for morning ablutions in his bedroom reveal his devout, highly disciplined nature.

Empress Elisabeth, or 'Sisi' as she is fondly nicknamed, whiled away many an hour penning poetry in the ruby-red **Stairs Cabinet**, and brushing up on various European languages while her ankle-length locks were tended in the privacy of her **dressing room**. Blue-and-white silk wall hangings adorn the **imperial bedroom** that Franz and Sisi sometimes shared. The neo-rococo **Empress' Salon** features portraits of some of Maria Theresia's 16 children, including Marie Antoinette in hunting garb, poignantly oblivious to her fate at the French guillotine in 1793. Laid with leaded crystal and fragile porcelain, the table in the **Marie Antoinette Room** is where Franz Josef used to dig into hearty meals of goulash and schnitzel (health-conscious Sisi preferred beef broth and strawberries out of view).

More portraits of Maria Theresia's brood fill the **Children's Room** and the **Balcony Room**, graced with works by court painter Martin van Meytens. Keep an eye out for the one of ill-fated daughter **Maria Elisabeth**, considered a rare beauty before she contracted smallpox. The disease left her so disfigured that all hope of finding a husband vanished, and she entered convent life.

In the exquisite white-and-gold **Mirror Room**, a six-year-old Mozart performed for a rapturous

www.schoenbrunn.at

13, Schönbrunner Schlossstrasse 47

adult/child Imperial Tour €13.30/9.80, Grand Tour €16.40/10.80, Grand Tour with guide €19.40/12.30

⏲ 8.30am-6.30pm Jul & Aug, to 5.30pm Sep, Oct & Apr-Jun, to 5pm Nov-Mar

☑ Top Tip

▶ Don't miss a wander around pretty Hietzing's shops, wine bars and restaurants.

✖ Take a Break

Head to **Pure Living Bakery** (www.pureliving-bakery.com; 13, Altgasse 12; cakes & snacks €4-10.50; ⏲ 9am-9pm; 🍴) for coffee and cake or lunch.

Grab a bottle of Austrian wine from **1130Wein** (www.1130wein.at; Lainzerstrasse 1; ⏲ 10am-7pm Mon-Fri, to 3pm Sat) for a Schloss picnic.

Maria Theresia in 1762. According to his father Leopold, 'Wolferl leapt onto Her Majesty's lap, threw his arms around her neck and planted kisses on her face.' Fairest of all, however, is the 40m-long **Great Gallery**, where the Habsburgs threw balls and banquets, a frothy vision of stucco, mirrors and gilt chandeliers, topped with a fresco by Italian artist Gregorio Guglielmi showing the glorification of Maria Theresia's reign. Decor aside, this was where the historic meeting between John F Kennedy and Soviet leader Nikita Khrushchev took place in 1961.

Wandering through the porcelain-crammed **Chinese Cabinets** brings you to the equestrian fanfare of the **Carousel Room** and the **Hall of Ceremonies**, with five monumental paintings showing the marriage of Joseph, heir to the throne, to Isabella of Parma in 1760. Mozart, only four at the time of the wedding, was added as an afterthought by the artist, who took several years to complete the picture, by which time the virtuoso was a rising star.

If you have a Grand Tour ticket, continue through to the palace's **east wing**. Franz Stephan's apartments begin in the sublime **Blue Chinese Salon**, where the intricate floral wall paintings are done on Chinese rice paper. The jewel-box *pietra dura* tables, inlaid with semi-precious stones, are stellar examples of Florentine craftsmanship. The negotiations that led to the collapse of the Austro-Hungarian Empire in 1918 were held here. A century before, Napoleon chose Schönbrunn as his HQ when he occupied Vienna in 1805 and 1809

and the **Napoleon Room** was where he may have dreamed about which country to conquer next. Look for the portrait of his only legitimate son, the Duke of Reichstadt.

Passing through the rosewood **Millions Room**, the **Gobelin Salon**, filled with Flemish tapestries, and the **Red Salon** brimming with Habsburg portraits, you reach Maria Theresia's **bedroom**, with a throne-like red velvet and gold embroidered four-poster bed. Franz Josef was born here in 1830. Portraits of the Habsburgs hang on the walls of Archduke Franz Karl's **study**, and the tour ends in the **Hunting Room**, with paintings noting Schönbrunn's origins as a hunting lodge.

Gardens

The beautifully tended formal **gardens** (admission free; ⏱6.30am–dusk) are appealing whatever the season. The grounds, which were opened to the public in 1779, hide a number of attractions in the tree-lined avenues that were arranged according to a grid and star-shaped system between 1750 and 1755. From 1772 to 1780 Ferdinand Hetzendorf added some of the final touches under the instructions of Joseph II: fake **Roman ruins** (adult/child €3.60/2.80) in 1778; the **Neptunbrunnen** (Neptune Fountain; adult/child €3.60/2.80), an equally empire-boosting Greek-mythology-themed folly in 1781; and the crowning glory, the **Gloriette** (adult/child €3.60/2.80; ⏱9am–6pm, closed early Nov–mid-Mar), in 1775. The view from the Gloriette is, as the name suggests, glorious.

SCHLOSS SCHÖNBRUNN & GARDENS

The original **Schöner Brunnen**, from which the palace got its name, now pours through the stone pitcher of a nymph near the Roman ruins. The 630m-long **Irrgarten** (Maze; adult/child €5.30/3; ☺8.30am-5.30pm) is a classic design based on the original maze that occupied its place from 1720 to 1892; adjoining this is the **Labyrinth**, a playground with games, climbing equipment and a giant mirror kaleidoscope.

To the east is the **Kronprinzengarten** (Privy Garden; adult/student & child €3.60/2.80), a replica of the garden that occupied the space around 1750.

Kindermuseum

Schönbrunn's **Children's Museum** (www. kaiserkinder.at/kindermuseum.html; adult/ child €8.80/6.70; ☺10am-5pm) does what it knows best: imperialism. Activities and displays help kids discover the day-to-day life of the Habsburg court; they then don princely or princessly outfits and start ordering the serfs (parents) around. Other rooms devoted to toys, natural science and archaeology all help to keep them entertained. **Guided tours** in German are a regular feature, departing at 10.30am, 1.30pm and 3pm (in English by appointment only).

Marionetten Theater

This small **theatre** (☎01-817 32 47; www. marionettentheater.at; tickets full performances adult €11-39, child €9-25; ☺box office on performance days from 11am) puts on marionette performances of the much-loved

Irrgarten (Maze; p119)

productions *The Magic Flute* (2½ hours) and *Aladdin* (1¼ hours). They're a delight for kids young, old and in between. The puppet costumes are exceptionally ornate and eye-catching.

Wagenburg

The **Wagenburg** (Imperial Coach Collection; www.kaiserliche-wagenburg.at; adult/child €8/ free; ☺9am-5pm mid-Mar–Nov, 10am-4pm Dec–mid-Mar) displays a vast array of carriages, including Emperor Franz Stephan's coronation carriage, with its ornate gold plating, Venetian glass panes and painted cherubs. The whole thing weighs an astonishing 4000kg. Also look for the dainty child's carriage built for Napoleon's son.

Schönbrunn Zoo

Founded in 1752 as a menagerie by Franz Stephan, the Schönbrunn **Tiergarten** (www.zoovienna.at; adult/child €18.50/9; ☺9am-6.30pm high season, to 4.30pm low season) is the world's oldest zoo. It houses some 750 animals, including giant pandas, emus, armadillos and Siberian tigers. Feeding times are staggered throughout the day – maps on display tell you who's dining when. The zoo's layout is reminiscent of a bicycle wheel, with pathways as spokes and an octagonal pavilion at its centre. The pavilion dates from 1759 and was used as the imperial breakfast room.

Wüstenhaus

The small **Wüstenhaus** (Desert House; 📞01-877 92 94 390; 13, Maxingstrasse 13b; adult/child €6/4.50; ⏰9am-6pm May-Sep, to 5pm Oct-Apr) makes good use of the once disused Sonnenuhrhaus (Sundial House) to re-create arid desert scenes. There are four sections – Northern Africa and the Middle East, Africa, the Americas and Madagascar – with rare cacti and live desert animals. A combined ticket for the Palmenhaus and Wüstenhaus costs €6.

Palmenhaus

The **Palm House** (13, Maxingstrasse 13b; adult/child €6/4.50; ⏰9.30am-6.30pm May-Sep, to 5pm Oct-Apr; 🚇10, 58, 60) was built in 1882 by Franz Segenschmid as a replica of the one in London's Kew Gardens. Inside is a veritable jungle of tropical plants from around the world.

Tickets for Schloss Schönbrunn

If you plan to see several sights at Schönbrunn, it's worth purchasing one of the combined tickets. Prices vary according to whether it's summer season (April to October) or winter. The best way to get a ticket is to buy it in advance online and print it yourself.

The summer season **Classic Pass** (adult/under 19 years €21.60/13.40) is valid for a Grand Tour of Schloss Schönbrunn (including all 40 rooms open to the public) and visits to the Kronprinzengarten (Crown Prince Garden), Irrgarten (Maze) and Labyrinth, Gloriette with viewing terrace, and **Hofbacksstube Schönbrunn** (Court

Bakery Schönbrunn; 📞01-24 100-300; per person incl strudel/coffee & strudel €5/10; ⏰10am-5pm Apr-Oct, to 4pm Nov-Mar, shows on the hour), with the chance to watch apple strudel being made and enjoy the result with a cup of coffee. A **Classic Pass 'light'** (adult/under 19 years €13.90/9.50) excludes the apple strudel show. The Court Bakery Schönbrunn can be viewed separately (it's inside Café Residenz).

The summer **Gold Pass** (adult/under 19 years €55.50/30.50) includes the Grand Tour, Crown Prince Garden, Tiergarten, Palmenhaus, Wüstenhaus, Wagenburg, Gloriette, Maze and Labyrinth, and Court Bakery Schönbrunn.

Nearby: Technisches Museum

The **Technisches Museum** (Technical Museum; www.technischesmuseum.at; 14, Mariahilfer Strasse 212; adult/under 19yr €12/free; ⏰9am-6pm Mon-Fri, 10am-6pm Sat & Sun; 🚇52, 58 Winckelmannstrasse) is dedicated to science, technology and engineering. There are many hands-on gadgets allowing you to conduct experiments, but the most interesting aspect is its historical collection. There's a Mercedes Silver Arrow from 1950, a model-T Ford from 1923 and penny-farthing bicycles to name a few.

Its small musical-instrument collection focuses mainly on keyboard instruments. The permanent exhibition is complemented by temporary ones; anyone with an engineering bent will absolutely love it here, as will two- to six-year-olds, for the well-thought-out Das Mini section.

The Best of
Vienna

Vienna's Best Walks

Essential Vienna 124

Living History 126

Vienna's Best...

Coffee Houses 128

Food 130

Drinking & Nightlife 132

Entertainment 134

Architecture 136

Guided Tours 137

Activities 138

For Free 139

For Kids 140

Art 141

Shopping 142

Kunsthistorisches Museum (p56)
MIKE CLEGG/500PX ©

Best Walks
Essential Vienna

🏃 The Walk

Vienna's grandeur unfolds in all its glory on this city stroll, from the timeless elegance of its Kaffeehäuser (coffee houses) to its monumental Hofburg palace, museums, parks and opulent opera house, as well as magnificent churches. This walk takes you past the city's greatest highlights.

Start Café Central

Finish [U]Herrengasse

Length 3.4km; 4 hours

✕ Take a Break

Café Central is a grand spot for coffee. Other good spots along this route include **Café Sacher** (p33), famed for its Sacher Torte, which Emperor Franz Josef loved, and **Café Mozart** (☎01-241 00-200; www. cafe-mozart.at; 01, Albertinaplatz 2; mains €15.90-32, cakes & pastries €4.50-8.50; ⏲kitchen 11.30am-11.30pm, bar 8am-midnight; 🛜; [U]Karlsplatz), which serves an array of cakes along with heartier Viennese meals.

EMI CRISTEA/SHUTTERSTOCK ©

Hofburg

❶ Café Central

Enjoy coffee and chocolate-truffle Altenbergtorte cake at **Café Central** (p34), adorned with marble pillars, arched ceilings and chandeliers. Stroll southeast on Herrengasse and go through Michaelertor gate to the Hofburg.

❷ Hofburg

The seat of the Habsburgs from 1273 to 1918, the **Hofburg** (p24), is a cross-section of history. Its oldest section is the 13th-century Schweizerhof (Swiss Courtyard), but other sections were added by new rulers.

❸ MuseumsQuartier

Former imperial stables now house the **MuseumsQuartier** (p62), an ensemble of museums, restaurants and bars spanning over 60,000 sq metres. Walking along its laneways, passing the **Leopold Museum** (p63) and **Kinder Museum** (p119), brings you out at Vienna's longest shopping street, Mariahilfer Strasse.

❹ Burggarten

One of Vienna's loveliest parks, the **Burggarten** (www.bmlfuw.gv.at/ministerium/bundesgaerten; 01, Burgring; ⏰6am-10pm Apr-Oct, 7.30am-5.30pm Nov-Mar; Ⓜ Museumsquartier, jD, 1, 2, 46, 49, 71 Burgring) is ideal for a stroll. Look for the **statues of Mozart** and **Emperor Franz Josef**. Don't miss the **Schmetterlinghaus** (Butterfly House; 533 85 70; www.schmetterlinghaus. at; adult/child €6.50/3.50; ⏰10am-4.45pm Mon-Fri, to 6.15pm Sat & Sun Apr-Oct, 10am-3.45 Nov-Mar), and the **Palmenhaus** (p121).

❺ Staatsoper

When Vienna's foremost opera and ballet venue, the **Staatsoper** (p78), was built in the 1860s, it was derided by the public and nicknamed the 'stone turtle'. Performances here are unforgettable; you can also go on a guided tour.

❻ Stephansdom

The nickname Steffl (Little Stephan) certainly doesn't fit this soaring Gothic masterpiece, the **Stephansdom** (p40). A church has stood here since the 12th century;

reminders include the Romanesque Riesentor (Giant Gate) and Heidentürme. A magnificent 1515-sculpted-stone pulpit presides inside.

❼ Peterskirche

Peterskirche (www.peterskirche.at; 01, Petersplatz; ⏰7am-8pm Mon-Fri, 9am-9pm Sat & Sun; Ⓤ Stephansplatz) was built in 1733 according to plans by Johann Lukas von Hildebrandt. Highlights include a fresco on the dome by JM Rottmayr and a golden altar depicting the martyrdom of St John of Nepomuk.

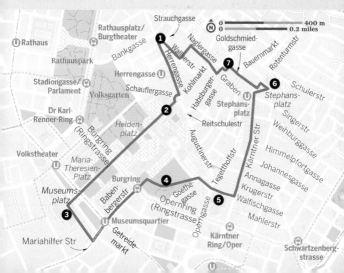

Best Walks
Living History

🏃 The Walk

Vienna's history comes to life along this stroll through the city's historic centre. From the Roman remains of Vindobona (Roman Vienna), it takes you past Vienna's main synagogue, historic churches, and poignant monument to the victims of fascism.

Start Römer Museum; Ⓤ Stephansplatz

Finish Dominikanerkirche; Ⓤ Stephansplatz

Length 1.8km; 2 hours

🍴 Take a Break

Dating from 1447 and frequented by Beethoven, Brahms, Schubert and Strauss, among others, Vienna's oldest restaurant, **Griechenbeisl** (p48), has vaulted rooms and a figure of Augustin trapped at the bottom of a well inside the front door. Every classic Viennese dish is on the menu (plus vegetarian options). Its warren of rooms include the oldest section, the Zither Stüberl, and the Mark Twain Zimmer, inscribed with the autographs of Twain and others.

ANNA LURYE/SHUTTERSTOCK ©

Ankeruhr

❶ Römer Museum

Vienna's Roman history is on show at the **Römer Museum** (01, Hoher Markt 3; adult/child €7/free; ⏰9am-6pm Tue-Sun; 🚌1A, 3A Hoher Markt, Ⓜ Stephansplatz). These ruins from the 1st to 5th centuries are thought to be part of the officers' quarters of the Roman legion camp at Vindobona. There are crumbled walls, an exhibition of artefacts and a 3D film (subtitled in English).

❷ Ankeruhr

The Hoher Markt is Vienna's oldest square and home to the **Ankeruhr** (Anker Clock; 01, Hoher Markt 10-11; Ⓜ Stephansplatz, Schwedenplatz) clock. Over a 12-hour period, figures including Roman Emperor Marcus Aurelius pass across the clock face. At noon, they all trundle past to the tune of organ music.

❸ Stadttempel

Vienna's main synagogue was completed in 1826 after reforms by Joseph II in the 1780s. Only Catholic places of worship were allowed to front major streets, so the **Stadt-**

tempel (p51) was built inside an apartment complex – the reason it was the sole survivor of 94 synagogues following the November Pogroms of 1938.

❹ Ruprechtskirche

Vienna's oldest church, **Ruprechtskirche** (St Rupert's Church; ☎01-535 60 03; www.ruprechtskirche. at; ⏰10am-noon Mon & Tues, 10am-noon & 3-5pm Wed, 10am-5pm Thu-Fri, 11.30am-3.30pm Sat; Ⓜ Schwedenplatz, Ⓑ1, 2 Schwedenplatz), is believed to date from 740. The lower levels date from the 12th century and the roof from the 15th century. The interior features a Romanesque nave from the 12th century.

❺ Morzinplatz

Located on the site of the former Gestapo HQ between Salztorbrücke and Marienbrücke, **Morzinplatz** (01; Ⓜ Schwedenplatz, Ⓑ1, 2 Schwedenplatz) is dominated by the **Monument to the Victims of Fascism**. It features the Star of David and the pink triangle, representing Jewish and homosexual victims of the Nazis.

❻ Dominikaner-kirche

Vienna's oldest baroque church, the **Dominikanerkirche** (☎01-512 91 74; 01 Postgasse 4; ⏰7am-7pm; Ⓜ Stubentor, Ⓑ1, 2 Stubentor), is largely the work of Italian architects and artisans. The Dominicans first came to Vienna in 1226, but their earliest church soon burned down. Its Gothic replacement was dismantled during the first Turkish siege in 1529 and its stone used to fortify the city walls.

Best
Coffee Houses

Vienna's long-standing tradition of coffee houses captures the spirit of *Gemütlichkeit* – that quintessential Austrian quality of cosiness and languid indulgence. Grand or humble, poster-plastered or chandelier-lit, this is where you can join the locals for coffee, cake and a slice of living history.

Coffee House Culture

In 2011 Vienna's coffee houses were added to the Unesco list of Intangible Cultural Heritage, which defines them as 'places where time and space are consumed, but only the coffee is found on the bill.' In 'Vienna's living rooms', the spirit of unhurried gentility remains sacrosanct. Meanwhile, a number of coffee houses are ushering in a new age of creativity.

Coffee Decoder

Brauner Black with a tiny splash of cream; comes in *gross* (large) or *klein* (small).

Einspänner Strong coffee with whipped cream, served in a glass.

Verlängerter *Brauner* lengthened with hot water.

Mocca Sometimes spelled *Mokka* or *Schwarzer* – black coffee.

Melange The Viennese classic: half-coffee, half-milk and topped with milk froth or whipped cream.

Kapuziner With more milk than coffee and perhaps a sprinkling of grated chocolate.

Eiskaffee Cold coffee with vanilla ice cream and whipped cream.

Maria Theresia With orange liqueur and whipped cream.

Türkische Comes in a copper pot with coffee grounds and sugar.

☑ Top Tips

▶ **Prices** Expect to pay between €2 and €5 for a coffee, between €3 and €6 for a slice of cake, and around €9 for a main.

▶ **Opening hours** Usually open around 8am, and close anywhere between 7pm and midnight (earlier on Sundays).

▶ **Meals** Many *Kaffeehäuser* also serve *Frühstuck* (breakfast) and a moderately priced lunchtime *Tagesteller* (dish of the day). Dishes are invariably hearty.

Café Sperl

Best Historic Coffee Houses

Café Sperl The real-deal coffee house: history, good food, games and faded grandeur. (p87)

Café Central A drop of opulence in vaulted, marble surrounds. (p34)

Café Leopold Hawelka Viennese character exudes from the walls of this convivial coffee house. (p34)

Demel Decadent cakes that once pleased the emperor,'s palate. (p33)

Best New-Wave Cafes

Supersense Locally roasted coffee and a cool concept shop. (p113)

Cafe Menta Nouveau-retro hangout. (p106)

Pure Living Bakery Boho-flavoured garden cafe near Schönbrunn. (p117)

Best Free Live Music

Café Central A pianist plays from 5pm to 10pm daily. (p34)

Café Prückel Piano music from 7pm to 10pm on Monday, Wednesday and Friday in 1950s surrounds. (p45)

Diglas Bag a cosy booth to hear piano music from 7pm to 10pm Thursday to Saturday. (p52)

Worth a Trip

Every Viennese coffee house ought to be just like the wood-panelled, poster-plastered, fantastically eccentric **Sperlhof** (02, Grosse Sperlgasse 41; ⊙4pm-1.30am; Ⓤ Taborstrasse), which opened in 1923. It still attracts a motley crowd of coffee sippers, daydreamers, billiard and ping-pong players and chess whizzes today.

Best
Food

HELEN CATHCART/LONELY PLANET ©

Dining in Vienna gives you a taste of the city's history, at its street stands sizzling up sausages, candlelit vaulted-cellar wine bars and earthy, wood-panelled *Beisln* (bistro pubs) serving goulash and *Wiener Schnitzel*; its present, at hip cafes, multiethnic markets and international eateries; and its future, at innovative spaces with a wave of exciting chefs pushing in new directions.

Viennese Specialities

Vienna has a strong repertoire of traditional dishes. One or two are variations on dishes from other regions. Classics include:

Schnitzel *Wiener Schnitzel* should always be crumbed veal, but pork is gaining ground in some places.

Goulash *Rindsgulasch* (beef goulash) is everywhere in Vienna but attains exquisite heights at Meierei im Stadtpark.

Tafelspitz Traditionally this boiled prime beef swims in the juices of locally produced *Suppengrün* (fresh soup vegetables), before being served with *Kren* (horseradish) sauce.

Beuschel Offal, usually sliced lung and heart with a slightly creamy sauce.

Backhendl Fried, breaded chicken, often called *steirisches Backhendl* (Styrian fried chicken).

Zwiebelrostbraten Slices of roast beef smothered in gravy and fried onions.

Schinkenfleckerln Oven-baked ham and noodle casserole.

Bauernschmaus Platter of cold meats.

☑ **Top Tips**

▶ **Prices** This guide refers to the cost of a two-course meal, excluding drinks.

€ under €15
€€ €15-30
€€€ over €30

▶ **Lunch specials** Most restaurants have an inexpensive lunch special (*Mittagsmenü* or *Tagesteller*) for around €7 to €11.

Best Desserts

Kaiserschmarrn Sweet pancake with raisins

Apfelstrudel Apple strudel

Marillenknödel Apricot dumplings

Best Dining Experiences

Steirereck im Stadtpark Vienna's class act by the Wien River. (p105)

Lingenhel Deli-shop-bar-restaurant in a 200-year-old house serving seasonal treats. (p109)

Plachutta The ultimate place for Viennese *Tafelspitz* (boiled beef). (p45)

Blue Mustard Incredible Vienna-inspired decor, adventurous cooking, a permanent food truck and cocktail pairings. (p32)

Griechenbeisl The history-soaked *Beisl* of your dreams. (p48)

Best Schnitzels

Figlmüller Bills itself as the home of the schnitzel. (p50)

Huth Gastwirtschaft Neo-*Beisln* that serves a superb *Wiener Schnitzel* with cranberry sauce and parsley potatoes. (p49)

Zum Alten Fassl *Beisl* in a residential setting with a private garden. (p87)

Best Goulash

Meierei im Stadtpark Some speak of the world's best. (p106)

Glacis Beisl Authentic goulash in the Museums-Quartier. (p74)

Vollpension Vegan goulash with potato and tofu. (p85)

Best Snacks

Trzesniewski Upmarket open-faced sandwiches. (p33)

Naschmarkt Market stalls and sit-down eateries galore. (p91)

Bitzinger Würstelstand am Albertinaplatz Iconic sausage stand opposite the opera. (p25)

Eis Greissler Organic ice cream with vegan options. (p86)

Worth a Trip

Guerilla-style **Punks** (☎0664 275 70 72; www.punks.wien; 08, Florianigasse 50; small plates €4.50) is shaking up an otherwise genteel neighbourhood. Patrick Müller, Anna Schwab and René Steindachner have 'occupied' a former wine bar and eschewed the usual refit or any form of interior decoration; the focus is, quite literally, on the kitchen, with a menu of inventive small dishes prepared behind the bar.

Best
Drinking & Nightlife

Vienna's drinking scene spans vaulted wine cellars here since Mozart's day to boisterous beer gardens, boho student dives and dressy cocktail bars, retro and rooftop bars. And with over 700 hectares of vineyards within its city limits, a visit to a *Heuriger* (wine tavern) is a quintessential Viennese experience.

LONELY PLANET/GETTY IMAGES ©

Grape & Grain

While wine is the chosen drink of the Viennese, beer features heavily in the city's cultural make-up. Try the following:

Blauburgunder Complex, fruity Pinot noir red.

Grüner Veltliner Strong, fresh white with hints of citrus and pear.

Riesling Fruity white with strong acidity.

Zweigelt Full-bodied red with intense cherry aromas.

Dunkel Thick dark beer with a very rich flavour.

Helles Lager with a bite – clear and lightly hoppy.

Pils Crisp, strong and often bitter Pilsner beer.

Märzen Red-coloured beer with a strong malt taste.

Zwickel Unfiltered beer with a cloudy complexion.

Schnäpse (schnapps) Fruit brandy; usually consumed after a meal.

Useful Websites

Falter (www.falter.at) Event and party listings.

Vienna Online (www.vienna.at) Keep track of club nights with this event calendar.

Tourist Info Wien (www.wien.info) Nightlife listings arranged by theme.

☑ Top Tips

▶ **Drink Prices** Standard beer prices range from €2 to €5, depending on the venue and location (central Vienna tends to be more expensive). A decent glass of local wine starts around €3. Expect to pay at least €7 for a simple mixed drink and around €9 and up for a cocktail.

▶ **Club Entry** Entry prices can and do vary wildly – from nothing to €20 – and depend on who's on the decks. Many small, intimate clubs offer free entry at least once a week.

Sekt Comptoir

Best Drinking & Nightlife

Loos American Bar Find a cosy alcove for a cocktail at Loos' 1908 classic. (p34)

Volksgarten ClubDiskothek Party in the park at this glam club near the Hofburg. (p34)

Brickmakers Pub & Kitchen Craft beers, ciders and pop-up guest chefs. (p74)

Palmenhaus Sip cocktails with great outdoor seating overlooking Burggarten. (p25)

Best Microbreweries

Siebensternbräu Cheery brewpub with hoppy beers and a warm-weather courtyard. (p75)

Wieden Bräu *Helles*, *Märzen* and hemp beers, plus summertime garden. (p88)

Salm Bräu Relaxed pick for home brews right by Schloss Belvedere. (p109)

1516 Brewing Company Unusual brews include blueberry. (p52)

Best Wine Bars

Vinothek W-Einkehr Superb Austrian wines. (p44)

Sekt Comptoir Effervescent bar with Burgenland *Sekt* (sparkling wine) near the Naschmarkt. (p81)

Esterházykeller Rustic cellar with wines from the Esterházy Palace. (p35)

Worth a Trip

A hidden wonderland, convivial local *Heuriger* **Wieninger** (☏01-292 41 06; www.heuriger-wieninger.at; 21, Stammersdorfer Strasse 78, Stammersdorf; ☺3pm-midnight Fri, noon-midnight Sat & Sun mid-Mar–late Apr, 3pm-midnight Thu & Fri, noon-midnight Sat & Sun late Apr–mid-Dec; ▢30A, ▢30, 31) has a magical lantern- and candle-lit garden draped with vines and a cosy, wood-panelled interior. Enjoy its light, fruity wines (mainly whites) alongside gourmet Austrian dishes.

Best
Entertainment

From opera, classical music and theatre to live rock or jazz, Vienna offers a wealth of entertainment opportunities. The capital is home to the German-speaking world's oldest theatre, the Burgtheater, as well as the famous Wiener Sängerknaben (Vienna Boys' Choir) and the Vienna Philharmonic Orchestra, which performs in the acoustically superb Musikverein.

JAVIER MARTIN/SHUTTERSTOCK ©

Opera

Vienna is a world capital for opera, and a stroll down Kärntner Strasse from Stephansplatz to the Staatsoper will turn up more Mozart lookalikes (costumed ticket sellers) than you can poke a baton at. The two main performance spaces are the Staatsoper, which closes in July and August, and Theater an der Wien, which remains open during these months.

Classical Music

Opportunities to listen to classical music in Vienna abound. Churches are a hub for recitals of Bach and Händel especially, but also great venues for all sorts of classical music recitals.

Rock & Jazz

Vienna's rock and jazz scene is lively, with a strong local list as well as international acts playing from the smallest bars to the largest arenas. See **Falter** (www.falter.at) for bands, venues and dates. The biggest bashes are the **Donauinselfest** (https://donauinselfest.at; admission free; ⏲late Jun) and **Jazz Fest Wien** (www.viennajazz.org; ⏲late Jun–mid-Jul).

☑ **Top Tips**

▶ **Standing-room tickets** Check with concert venues including at the Staatsoper and Musikverein for details of purchasing standing-room tickets for just a few euros.

▶ **Theatre** Performances are invariably in German aside from Vienna's English Theatre.

Staatsoper

Best Entertainment

Staatsoper One of the world's foremost opera houses. (p78)

Musikverein Home of the Vienna Philharmonic Orchestra. (p89)

Hofburg Concert Halls The sumptuous Festsaal and Redoutensaal are regularly used for Strauss and Mozart concerts. (p35)

Radiokulturhaus Expect anything from odes to Sinatra and R.E.M. to evenings dedicated to Beethoven and Mozart. (p110)

Konzerthaus Major venue in classical-music circles. (p110)

Burgtheater

POSZTOS/SHUTTERSTOCK ©

Worth a Trip

Baroque-meets-contemporary concert hall **MuTh** (☎01-347 80 80; www.muth.at; 02, Obere Augartenstrasse 1e; Vienna Boys' Choir Fri performance €39-89; ⏱4-6pm Mon-Fri & 1 hour before performances; Ⓤ Taborstrasse) is the striking new home of the Vienna Boys' Choir's Friday afternoon choral sessions. The 400-seat auditorium also stages a top-drawer roster of dance, drama, opera, classical, rock and jazz performances.

Best
Architecture

LONELY PLANET/GETTY IMAGES ©

Unwittingly, the Ottomans helped form much of Vienna's architectural make-up as seen today. The second Turkish siege saw the Habsburgs freed from the threat of war, and money previously spent on defence was poured into urban redevelopment, resulting in a frenzy of building in the baroque period in the 17th and early 18th centuries.

Neoclassical, Biedermeier & the Ringstrasse

From the 18th century (culminating in the 19th), Viennese architects – like those all over Europe – turned to a host of neoclassical architectural styles.

The end of the Napoleonic Wars and the ensuing celebration at the Congress of Vienna in 1815 ushered in the Biedermeier period (named after a satirical middle-class figure in a Munich paper). Viennese artists produced some extraordinary furniture during this period.

In the mid-19th century, Franz Josef I called for the fortifications to be demolished and replaced with a ring road lined with magnificent imperial buildings. Demolition of the old city walls began in 1857, and glorious buildings were created.

Best Architectural Splendours

Stephansdom This soaring cathedral dominates Vienna's historic centre. (p40)

Schloss Belvedere Vienna's most sublime baroque palace. (p94)

Hofburg Six and a half centuries of imperial history. (p24)

Schloss Schönbrunn Baroque architectural beauty, garden grandeur. (p116)

Rathaus Vienna's neo-Gothic City Hall is the Ringstrasse's crowning glory. (p72)

Best
Guided Tours

JÖRG HACKEMANN/SHUTTERSTOCK ©

Space and Place (http://spaceandplace.at) For the inside scoop on Vienna, join Eugene on one of his fun, quirky tours. The alternative line-up includes Vienna Ugly tours, homing in on the capital's ugly side, to Smells Like Wien Spirit, exploring the city through smell, and the sociable Coffeehouse Conversations.

Hot Rod City Tour (☑01-660 87 73; www.hotrod-citytour-wien.com; 01, Judengasse 4; 2hr tour per person €99-119; ◷10am-8pm Oct-May, 8am-10pm Jun-Sep; ⓤSchwedenplatz) These low-to-the-ground one-person mini hot rods set off in convoy and cover a circuit of the city in 1½ hours. Helmets, walkie-talkies and insurance are included; you'll need a valid driver's licence (foreign licences accepted).

Fiaker Carriage Rides (20min/40min/1hr tour €55/80/110) One of the most romantic ways to see Vienna is aboard a *Fiaker*, a traditional-style open carriage (seating up to four passengers) drawn by a pair of horses. Drivers generally speak English and will point out places of interest en route. Lines of horses, carriages and bowler-hatted drivers can be found at Stephansplatz, Albertinaplatz and Heldenplatz at the Hofburg.

Ring Tram (☑01-790 91 00; www.wienerlinien.at; 01, Schwedenplatz, Platform C; adult/child €9/4; ◷10am-5.30pm; ☐1, 2, ⓤSchwedenplatz) An alternative to a DIY tour of the Ringstrasse by public tram is this continuous 30-minute loop (no stops) with video screens and multilingual commentary.

Oldtimer Bus Tours (☑01-503 74 43 12; www.oldtimertours.at; 01, departure from Heldenplatz; tours adult/child €19/12; ◷May–mid-Oct; ☐D, 1, 2, 71 Burgring, ⓤMuseumsquartier) Vintage open-top (closed if rainy) coaches trundle around the city centre and occasionally up to the Wienerwald (Vienna Woods).

Vienna Explorer (☑01-890 96 82; www.viennaexplorer.com; 01, Franz-Josefs-Kai 45; ◷tours Easter-Oct, bike rental 8.30am-6pm year-round; ☐1, ⓤSchwedenplatz) This long-standing outfit is excellent for bike tours in Vienna itself (three hours; adult/child €29/14.50) and further afield; it also has Vienna city walking tours (2½ hours; €16/8). Bike rental available.

DDSG Blue Danube (☑01-588 80; www.ddsg-blue-danube.at; 01, Schwedenbrücke; 1½-hour tours adult/child €22/11; ◷10.30am-6.20pm Easter-Oct; ⓤSchwedenplatz) Boats cover a variety of cruise routes.

Best
Activities

CREATIVEMARC/SHUTTERSTOCK ©

Vienna is a cracking city for outdoor activities. The Wienerwald (Vienna Woods) to the west is criss-crossed with hiking and cycling trails, while the Danube, Alte Donau and Donauinsel to the east offer boating, swimming, cycling and more. There are over 1200km of designated cycle paths, and the city is dotted with parks, some big (the Prater), some small (Stadtpark).

Best Swimming & Watersports

Badeschiff (Map p46, E3; www.badeschiff.at; 01, Danube Canal; adult/child €5/2.50; ⏰8am-10pm May-Sep, bar 10am-1am year-round, kitchen 10am-10pm year-round; 🚊1, Ⓤ Schwedenplatz) Floating on the bank of the Danube, this central 28m-long lap pool has multiple decks with umbrella-shaded sun loungers.

Donauinsel (Danube Island; Ⓤ Donauinsel) The Danube Island is Vienna's aquatic playground, with sections of beach (don't expect much sand) for swimming, boating and water skiing.

Strandbad Alte Donau (22, Arbeiterstrandbadstrasse 91; adult/child €5.50/3; ⏰9am-8pm Mon-Fri & 8am-8pm Sat & Sun May–mid-Sep; Ⓤ Alte Donau) This bathing area's facilities include a restaurant, beach-volleyball court, playing field, slides and plenty of tree shade.

3 City Wave (Map p102, A4; www.3citywave.at; 03; Schwarzenbergplatz; ⏰10am-10pm Sun-Thu, to 11pm Fri & Sat mid-Jun–Sep; Ⓤ Stadtpark; Karlsplatz) This artificial wave in front of the Hochstrahlbrunnen fountain on Schwarzenbergplatz draws novices and pros alike.

Best Ice Skating

Wiener Eistraum (Map p70, G1; www.wiener-eistraum.at; 01, Rathaus-platz; adult/child from €4, pre-heated skate hire €7.50/5.50; ⏰9am-10pm late Jan–early Mar; 🚊D, 1, 2 Rathaus, Ⓤ Rathaus) In the heart of winter, Rathaus-platz transforms into two connected ice rinks covering a total of 8000 sq metres, complemented by DJs, food stands and *Glühwein* (mulled wine) bars. The skating path zigzags through the nearby park and around the entire square.

Wiener Eislaufverein (Map p102 B4; www.wev.or.at; 03, Lothringerstrasse 22; adult/child €7/6, boot hire €6.50; ⏰9am-8pm Sat-Mon, to 9pm Tue-Fri; 🚊D Schwarzenbergplatz, Ⓤ Stadtpark) At 6000 sq metres, the Wiener Eislaufverein is the world's largest open-air skating rink.

Best
For Free

Vienna offers a wealth of opportunities to experience the city for free, from strolls through the city streets soaking up the spectacular architecture to a number of free museums, exhibitions, public buildings, parks and churches, as well as fabulous free entertainment, festivals and events.

DINKASPELL/SHUTTERSTOCK ©

Free Museums & Exhibitions

Some museums are free for those under 19 years, and permanent exhibitions in all 20 of the municipal museums run by the City of Vienna (www.wienmuseum.at) are free on the first Sunday of the month.

Free Entertainment

Free festivals and events abound during summer, including rock, pop, folk and country performances, opera, operettas and concerts and films at outdoor cinemas.

In April, May, June and September and on Silvester (New Year's Eve), an open-air LED video wall sets up outside the Staatsoper, screening operatic performances, with 180 chairs set up for each broadcast.

Winter freebies include wandering the city's enchanting *Christkindlmärkte* (Christmas markets).

You can often hear DJs spinning for free in bars, and sometimes at open-air spaces such as the MuseumsQuartier.

Best Free Public Spaces

Stephansdom The northern side-aisle is free to visit. (p40)

Rathaus Vienna's splendid City Hall has free guided tours. (p72)

Prater Vienna's park and woodland across the Danube Canal. (p112)

Augarten Eighteenth-century parkland with paths and meadows. (p114)

Best
For Kids

Vienna is a wonderfully kid-friendly city. Children are welcomed in all aspects of everyday life, and many of the city's museums go out of their way to gear exhibitions towards children. Children's servings are typically available in restaurants, and, when kids need to burn off energy, playgrounds are plentiful.

NADYA EUGENE/SHUTTERSTOCK ©

Best Museums & Attractions for Kids

Haus der Musik Practical exhibits for almost all ages promote an understanding of music. (p48)

Naturhistorisches Museum Superb anthropology section where you can delve into forensics, plus overnight stays. (p66)

Technisches Museum Hands-on science and technology exhibits. (p121)

Zoom Exhibition sections and programs of hands-on arts and crafts. (p64)

Dschungel Wien Children's theatre with dance and occasional English performances. (p65)

Kindermuseum Kids can dress up as princes and princesses at Schloss Schönbrunn's Children's Museum. (p119)

Marionetten Theater Schloss Schönbrunn's puppet theatre enchants children. (p119)

Tiergarten Some 750 animals including giant pandas and Siberian tigers call Schönbrunn's zoo home. (p120)

☑ Top Tips

▶ **Public Transport** Free for children under six years; half-price on single tickets under 15 years.

▶ **Hotels** Cots (cribs) usually available. Children under 12 often stay free in their parents' room. Babysitters are best arranged through your hotel.

▶ **Babies** Nappy (diaper) changing facilities are rare in restaurants. Breastfeeding in public is fine.

Best
Art

KIEV.VICTOR/SHUTTERSTOCK ©

Vienna is one of the world's most fascinating capitals when it comes to the visual arts and architecture. The Habsburg monarchs fostered and patronised the arts in grand style, leaving a rich legacy of fine historic paintings and sculptures. You'll encounter them all over the city, complemented today by modern and contemporary works.

Jugendstil & the Secession

Vienna's branch of the Europe-wide Art Nouveau movement was known as *Jugendstil* ('Youthful Style'). By the second decade of the 20th century, many artists were moving towards a uniquely Viennese style, called Secession, which stripped away some of the more decorative aspects of *Jugendstil*. No one embraced the sensualism of *Jugendstil* and Secessionism more than Klimt, one of Vienna's most famous artists.

Contemporary Arts

Vienna has a thriving contemporary arts scene with a strong emphasis on confrontation, pushing boundaries and exploring new media. Standing in stark contrast to the more self-consciously daring movements such as Actionism, Vienna's extensive Neue Wilde group emphasises traditional techniques and media.

Best Museums & Galleries

Kunsthistorisches Museum Packed with Old Masters. (p56)

Albertina Exceptional collection of graphic art. (p30)

Schloss Belvedere Home to the world's largest Klimt collection. (p94)

Leopold Museum Vast collection of mainly 19th-century and modernist Austrian artworks. (p63)

MUMOK Vienna's finest collection of 20th-century art; Viennese Actionism is regularly displayed. (p63)

Secession At this showcase of the Secessionists, the biggest draw is Klimt's gilded *Beethoven Frieze*. (p84)

Best
Shopping

With a long-standing history of craftsmanship, in recent years this elegant city has spread its creative wings in the fashion and design world. Whether you're browsing for hand-painted porcelain in the Innere Stadt, new-wave streetwear in Neubau or epicurean treats in the Freihausviertel, you'll find inspiration, a passion for quality and an attentive eye for detail.

RAIMUND KOCH/GETTY IMAGES ©

Shopping Strips

Kärntner Strasse The Innere Stadt's main shopping street and a real crowd-puller.

Kohlmarkt A river of high-end glitz, flowing into a magnificent Hofburg view.

Neubau Track down the city's hottest designers along boutique-clogged streets like Kirchengasse, Lindengasse and Neubaugasse.

Mariahilfer Strasse Vienna's mile of high-street style, with big names and crowds.

Freihausviertel Lanes packed with home-grown fashion, design and speciality food stores, south of Naschmarkt.

Theobaldgasse Hole-in-the-wall shops purvey everything from fair-trade fashion to organic food.

Best Shopping

Steiff The original creator of the teddy bear. (p37)

Henzls Ernte Garden veg and foraged herbs go into delectable spreads, sugars and salts. (p81)

Dorotheum Hammer time at this giant treasure chest of an auction house. (p37)

Gabarage Upcycling Design Reborn cast-offs become cutting-edge design. (p91)

☑ **Top Tips**

▶ **Bargaining** Bargaining isn't accepted in shops, although you can certainly haggle when buying secondhand. It's a must at the *Flohmärkte* (flea markets).

▶ **Taxes** *Mehrwertsteuer* (MWST; value-added tax) is 20% for most goods. Non-EU visitors can claim a MWST refund on purchases over €75.01; check www.globalblue.com for details.

Survival Guide

Before You Go   **144**

When to Go 144
Book Your Stay 144

Arriving in Vienna   **145**

Vienna International Airport 145
Wien Hauptbahnhof 146

Getting Around   **147**

Bicycle. 147
Bus. 147
Taxi. 147
Train. 147
Tram. 148

Essential Information   **148**

Business Hours. 148
Discount Cards 148
Electricity. 149
Emergency 149
Internet Access 149
Money 149
Public Holidays 149
Safe Travel 150
Telephone. 150
Toilets 151
Tourist Information 151
Travellers with Disabilities 151
Visas. 151

Language   **152**

Survival Guide

Before You Go

When to Go

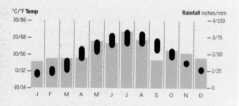

°C/°F Temp
Rainfall inches/mm

→ Spring (Apr–Jun) Mild
temperatures, emerging
greenery. Easter heralds
the start of Vienna's tourist season.

→ Summer (Jul–Aug)
Warm to hot weather,
riverside beaches. Many
restaurants, bars and
smaller shops close for
the *Sommerpause* (sum-
mer break).

→ Autumn (Sep–Oct)
Temperatures fall,
crowds tail off and
Goldener Oktober brings
autumnal colour.

→ Winter (Nov–Mar)
Often snowy; outdoor
skating rinks set up
across the city.

Book Your Stay

→ Vienna has an extensive
range of properties in
all price categories;
book ahead from Easter
through to September
and during special events
such as the Christmas
markets.

→ Vienna has a smatter-
ing of *Jugendherbergen*
(youth hostels), both
private and hostels af-
filiated with Hostelling
International (HI). In the
former, no membership is
required.

→ Midrange proper-
ties span homey, often
family-run *Pensionen*
(guesthouses), many
traditional to smart hotels
and apartments.

→ At the top end are luxury
establishments with chan-
deliers, antique furniture
and original 19th-century
oil paintings, along with
statement-making design
hotels.

→ Be aware that breakfast
isn't always included

in the overnight rate;
a coffee house or cafe
can often be a better-
value, more atmospheric
option.

Useful Websites

Lonely Planet (www.
lonelyplanet.com/aus-
tria/vienna/hotels) Re-
views of Lonely Planet's
top choices and online
booking.

**Hostelling Interna-
tional** (www.hihostels.
com) Global youth hostel
organisation.

Tourist Info Wien (www.
wien.info/en/hotels)
Vienna's tourist office.

Best Budget

**Hotel am Brillantengr-
und** (www.brillantengr-
und.com) Set around a
sociable courtyard.

my MOjO vie (www.
mymojovie.at) Hostel
with upbeat style.

Hotel Drei Kronen
(www.hotel3kronen.at)
Elegant pension serving
Sekt (sparkling wine) at
breakfast.

Pension Kraml (www.
pensionkraml.at) Spa-
cious rooms in a historic
pension.

Best Midrange

Hollmann Beletage
(www.hollmann-beletage.
at) Stylish hotel with
perks.

Hotel Kärntnerhof
(www.karntnerhof.com)
Viennese charm.

**Boutiquehotel
Stadthalle** (www.hotel-
stadthalle.at) Cosy and
eco-aware.

Spiess & Spiess (www.
spiess-vienna.at) Elegant,
well-located pension.

Hotel Capricorno (www.
schick-hotels.com/hotel-
capricorno) Shimmering
interiors and canal-side
balconies.

Best Top End

Grand Ferdinand Hotel
(www.grandferdinand.
com) With a rooftop infin-
ity pool.

**Radisson Blu Style
Hotel** (www.radissonblu.
com/stylehotel-vienna)
Ultrastylish design.

Hotel Imperial (www.
grandluxuryhotels.com)
Favourite for European
royalty.

DO & CO (www.docoho-
tel.com) Sexiest hotel in
the centre.

Arriving in Vienna

Vienna International Airport

Located 19km southwest
of the city centre, **Vienna
International Airport**
(Map p102, E3; VIE; 01-700
722 233; www.viennaairport.
com;) operates ser-
vices worldwide. Facilities
include restaurants and
bars, banks and ATMs,
money-exchange coun-
ters, supermarkets, a
post office, car-hire agen-
cies and two left-luggage
counters open 5.30am
to 11pm (per 24 hours
€4 to €8; maximum
six-month storage). Bike
boxes (€35) and baggage
wrapping (per item €12)
are available.

Train

The **City Airport Train**
(CAT; www.cityairporttrain.
com; single/return €11/19)
departs from Vienna
International Airport
every 30 minutes from
6.09am to 11.30pm,
and from Wien-Mitte
train station every 30
minutes from 5.36am to
11.06pm. Journey time is
15 minutes.

The S7 (www.oebb.at; €4.40, 25 minutes) does the same journey to/from the airport. It runs from 4.48am to 12.18am from the airport to Wien-Mitte, and from 4.19am to 11.49pm from Wien-Mitte to the airport.

Bus

Vienna Airport Lines (☎01-700 732 300; www.postbus.at; ☉8am-7.30pm Mon-Sat) has three services connecting different parts of Vienna with the airport. The most central is the **Vienna Airport Lines bus stop** at Morzinplatz/Schwedenplatz (bus 1185; one way/return €8/13, 20 minutes), running via the Wien-Mitte train station.

Taxi

A taxi to/from the airport costs between €25 and €50. The yellow **Taxi 40100** (☎01-401 00; www.taxi40100.at) in the arrival hall (near the bookshop) has a fixed airport rate of €36. **C&K Airport Service** (☎01-444 44; www.cundk.at) has rates starting at €33.

Wien Hauptbahnhof

Vienna's main train station (Map p82, H5), 3km south of Stephansdom, handles all international trains as well as trains from all of Austria's provincial capitals and many local and regional trains.

➡ **S-Bahn** S-Bahn lines S1, S2 and S3 connect Hauptbahnhof with Wien Meidling, Wien-Mitte and Praterstern.

➡ **U-Bahn** U1 serves Karlsplatz and Stephansplatz.

➡ **Tram** O to Praterstern, 18 to Westbahnhof and Burggasse/Stadthalle. Tram D connects Hauptbahnhof-Ost with the Ringstrasse.

➡ **Bus** 13A runs through Vienna's *Vorstädte* (inner suburbs) Margareten, Mariahilf, Neubau and Josefstadt, all between the Ringstrasse and the Gürtel.

Tickets & Passes

Tickets and passes for **Wiener Linien** (☎01-7909-100; www.wienerlinien.at) services (U-Bahn, trams and buses) can be purchased at U-Bahn stations and on trams and buses, in a Tabakladen (Trafik; tobacco kiosk), as well as from a few staffed ticket offices.

Single Ticket *(Einzelfahrschein)* €2.20; good for one journey, with line changes; costs €2.30 if purchased on trams and buses (correct change required).

24-/48-/72-hour Tickets *(24-/48-/72-Stundenkarten)* €7.60, €13.30 and €16.50 respectively. Require validation.

Eight-day Ticket *(8-Tage-Klimakarte)* €38.40; valid for eight days, not necessarily consecutive; validate the card as and when you need it.

Weekly Ticket *(Wochenkarte)* €16.20; valid Monday to Sunday only (ie tickets purchased on a Friday are still only valid to the Sunday).

Senior Citizens Over 60s can buy a €2.80 ticket valid for two trips; enquire at transport information offices.

Getting Around

Bicycle

Vienna is a fabulous place to cycle. Bikes can be carried for free on carriages marked with a bike symbol on S-Bahns and U-Bahns from 9am to 3pm and after 6.30pm Monday to Friday, after 9am Saturday and all day Sunday. It's not possible to take bikes on trams or buses.

Citybike Wien (Vienna City Bike; www.citybikewien. at; 1st/2nd/3rd hr free/€1/2, per hr thereafter €4) Over 120 bike-share stands are located across the city. A credit card and €1 registration fee is required to hire bikes; just swipe your card and follow the instructions. The bikes are intended as an alternative to transport and can only be locked up at a bike station (unless you use your own lock). A lost bike will cost you €600.

Bus

Bus connections can be useful for outlying parts of town or for travellers with limited physical mobility.

Regular buses Bus 13A runs north–south through the *Vorstädte* between Hauptbahnhof and Alser Strasse. 2A connects Schwarzenbergplatz, Stephansplatz, Schwedenplatz and Michaelerplatz. 3A connects Börsenplatz and Schottentor with Stephansplatz and Stubentor. Most lines run from 5am to midnight, with fewer (sometimes nonexistent) services on weekends.

Night buses *Nightline* routes cover much of the city and run every half-hour from 12.30am to 5am. Note that after midnight on Friday and Saturday the U-Bahn runs all night. Schwedenplatz, Schottentor and Kärntner Ring/Oper are stopping points for many night bus services; look for buses and bus stops marked with 'N'. All transport tickets are valid for *Nightline* services. N25 runs around the Ringstrasse then via Schwedenplatz, Leopoldstadt to Kagraner Platz and beyond weekdays.

Taxi

Taxis are reliable and relatively cheap by Western European standards. City journeys are metered; the minimum charge is roughly €3.80 from 6am to 11pm Monday to Saturday and €4.30 any other time, plus a per-kilometre fee of €1.42. A telephone reservation costs an additional €2.80. A tip of 10% is expected. Taxis are easily found at train stations and taxi stands all over the city. To order one, contact **Taxi 40100** (☏01-401 00; www.taxi40100.at) or **Willkommen Taxi** (☏01-60 160; www.taxi60160.at). These accept common credit and debit cards (check before hopping in).

Train

U-Bahn The U-Bahn is a quick, efficient and inexpensive way of getting around the city. There are five lines: U1 to U4 and U6 (construction on the U5 starts in 2018). Stations have lifts as well as escalators. Platforms have timetable information and signs showing the exits and nearby facilities. The U-Bahn runs from 5am to midnight Monday to Thursday and continuously from Friday through to Sunday night.

Vienna's Districts

The 23 *Wiener Bezirke* (Vienna districts) spiral out clockwise from the centre (although some leap-frog position). The Innere Stadt (01) sits at the centre, encircled by Ringstrasse. Roughly between Ringstrasse and the Gürtel ring road are the *Vorstädte* (inner suburbs): 02 to 09. Outside the Gürtel are the *Vororte* (outer suburbs): 10 to 20. Districts 21 and 22 are on the city's northeastern flank, while 23 sits on the southwestern edge.

Every address in Vienna begins with the district number, with street numbers starting closest to the city. The district number is formed by the middle two digits of its four-digit post code (1010 is the 01).

U-Bahns and trams get you close to most sights, especially in the centre and fringing Vorstadt areas (ie between the Ringstrasse and Gürtel).

S-Bahn S-Bahn trains, designated by a number preceded by an 'S', operate on 10 lines and service the suburbs or satellite towns. Trains run from 4.30am to 1.10am. For travel outside of Vienna and outside of the ticket zone, you'll have to purchase an extension on your standard ticket or buy a ticket from a machine at the station; check on maps posted in train stations.

Tram

Vienna's tram network has 29 lines, and it's the perfect way to view the city on the cheap. Trams are either numbered or lettered (eg 1, 2, D) and cover the city centre and some suburbs. Services run from 5.15am to 11.45pm.

Essential Information

Business Hours

Many restaurants, bars, entertainment venues and smaller shops shut in July/August.

Banks 8am or 9am to 3pm Monday to Friday, to 5.30pm on Thursday. Smaller branches close for lunch.

Post offices 8am to noon and 2pm to 6pm Monday to Friday; some also open Saturday morning. The **main post office** (www.post.at; 01, Fleischmarkt 19; ⏰7am-10pm Mon-Fri, 9am-10pm Sat & Sun; 🚈1, 2, Ⓤ Schwedenplatz) has extended hours.

Pubs & clubs Vary.

Restaurants Generally 11am to 2pm and 6pm to 10pm or 11pm.

Shops Usually open 9am to 6.30pm Monday to Friday (some to 9pm Thursday or Friday) and until 5pm Saturday.

Supermarkets All close Sunday.

Discount Cards

Vienna Card (*Die Wien-Karte;* 48/72 hours €21.90/24.90) Unlimited travel on public transport (including night buses) and hundreds of discounts at selected museums, cafes, *Heurigen* (wine taverns), restaurants and shops, and on guided tours and the City Airport Train (CAT). The discount usually amounts to 5% to 25% off the normal price. Purchased at **Tourist Info Wien** (Map p28, F5; 📞01-245 55; www.wien.info; 01, Albertinaplatz; ⊙9am-7pm; 🛜; 🚃D, 1, 2, 71 Kärntner Ring/Oper, Ⓤ Stephansplatz), the **Airport Information Office** (⊙7am-10pm) and many concierge desks at the top hotels.

Electricity

230V/50Hz

Emergency

In case of emergency, the general number for ambulance, fire and police is 📞112.

Ambulance 📞144
(Rettung)

Fire (Feuerwehr) 📞122

Police (Polizei) 📞133

Internet Access

Virtually all hostels and hotels in Vienna offer free wi-fi, called WLAN (pronounced vee-lan) in German. Many cafes, coffee houses and bars also offer free wi-fi; check locations at www.freewave.at/en/hotspots.

The city's over 400 free hotspots are mapped on www.wien.gv.at/stadtplan. Search for 'wien.at Public WLAN', accept the terms and connect.

Alternatively, if your phone is unlocked, you can purchase a pre-paid SIM card with a data allowance from phone shops, kiosks and *tabakladen*.

Money

→ Austria uses the euro (€). For updated exchange rates, check www.xe.com.

→ ATMs are widely available.

→ Credit cards are not always accepted in budget hotels or budget-to-midrange restaurants. Bars and cafes usually only accept cash.

→ Many automated services, such as ticket machines, require a chip-and-PIN credit card (even some foreign chip-enabled cards won't work). Ask your bank for advice before you leave.

Public Holidays

The only establishments remaining open on holidays are bars, cafes and restaurants. Museums are usually open except for New Year's Day, Christmas Day and sometimes May Day. The big school break is July and August; most families go away during this time, so the city is quieter, but the downside is that a high percentage of restaurants and entertainment venues close.

New Year's Day (Neujahr) 1 January

Epiphany (Heilige Drei Könige) 6 January

Easter Monday (Ostermontag) March or April

Labour Day (Tag der Arbeit) 1 May

Ascension Day (Christi Himmelfahrt) Sixth Thursday after Easter

Whit Monday (Pfingstmontag) Sixth Monday after Easter

Corpus Christi (Fronleichnam) Second Thursday after Pentecost

Assumption (Maria Himmelfahrt) 15 August

National Day (Nationalfeiertag) 26 October

All Saints' Day (Allerheiligen) 1 November

Immaculate Conception (Mariä Empfängnis) 8 December

Christmas Eve (Heiligabend) 24 December; everything closed afternoon

Christmas Day (Christfest) 25 December

St Stephen's Day (Stephanitag) 26 December

Safe Travel

Vienna is a very safe city and in general women and men will have no trouble walking around at night.

➡ Karlsplatz station and Gumpendorfer Strasse can be boisterous late in the evening.

➡ The Prater and Praterstern can get dodgy at night. Ausstellungsstrasse is best avoided due street walkers and kerb-crawlers.

➡ The Gürtel has a sprinkling of red-light clubs: north of Westbahnhof along the Neubaugürtel has a high concentration (with fewer around Thaliastrasse), and directly south to Gumpendorfer Strasse can be seedy.

➡ S-Bahn and tram stops along Margareten and Wiedner Gürtel can be edgy.

Telephone

Country code Austria's country code is ☎ 0043.

Area code Vienna's area code is ☎ 01. When calling from overseas drop the zero in the Vienna code.

Roaming Network works on GSM 1800 and is compatible with GSM 900 phones. US cell phones will only work here if they are at least tri-band. Japanese phones need to be quad-band (world phone).

Prepaid SIM cards Phone shops, kiosks and Tabakladen (tabacconists) sell prepaid SIM cards for phone calls and data. To use one, your phone needs to be unlocked.

Data roaming Make sure the data transfer capabili-

Dos & Don'ts

The Viennese are fairly formal and use irony to alleviate social rules and constraints.

Greetings Grüss Gott or the less formal Servus! are the usual forms of greeting; Guten Tag is also common. Stick to the polite Sie (you) form unless you know someone well or are of a similar age in a young-ish scene. Never use du with shop assistants or waiters.

Acknowledgements When entering a breakfast room, it's usual to acknowledge others by saying Guten Morgen when you walk in and Auf Wiedersehen on leaving.

Telephone Give your name at the start of a telephone call, especially when making reservations. When completing the call, say Auf Wiederhören ('goodbye'; customary form on phone).

ty is deactivated while you are roaming. Austria has lots of wi-fi hotspots for surfing on smart phones with wi-fi capability.

Toilets

➡ Large shopping centres have facilities that are free.

➡ Facilities at U-Bahn stations and public places marked by a 'WC' sign usually incur a small charge (around €0.50).

➡ Museums reliably have good, clean facilities.

➡ At cafes and bars, facilities are only for paying customers; ask first or consider ordering a coffee.

Tourist Information

Tourist Info Wien (Map p28; ☏ 01-245 55; www. wien.info; 01, Albertinaplatz; ☺ 9am-7pm; ☎; ☒ D, 1, 2, 71 Kärntner Ring/Oper, ⓤ Stephansplatz) Vienna's main tourist office.

Airport Information Office (☺ 7am-10pm)

Travellers with Disabilities

Vienna is increasingly well geared for people with disabilities (*Behinderte*). Ramps are common (though by no means

ubiquitous). Most U-Bahn stations have wheelchair lifts. All U-Bahn stations have guiding strips for the blind. All buses these days have ramps (the driver will assist) and tilt technology, and most of the trams in service have low-floor access allowing entry in a wheelchair; this will rise to 100% of trams in 2017. Traffic lights 'bleep' to indicate when pedestrians can safely cross the road.

Resources

Tourist Info Wien (Map p28; ☏ 01-245 55; www. wien.info; 01, Albertinaplatz; ☺ 9am-7pm; ☎; ☒ D, 1, 2, 71 Kärntner Ring/Oper, ⓤ Stephansplatz) Your source for advice and information. Its detailed booklet *Accessible Vienna*, in German or English, provides information on hotels and restaurants with disabled access, plus addresses of hospitals, medical-equipment shops, parking places, toilets and more. Download it at www. wien.info/en/travel-info/ accessible-vienna.

Lonely Planet Download Lonely Planet's free Accessible Travel guide from http://lptravel.to/ AccessibleTravel.

Bizeps (☏ 01-523 89 21; www.bizeps.at; 02, Schönn-gasse 15-17, Vienna; ⓤ Messe-Prater) A centre providing support and self-help for people with disabilities. Located two blocks north of Messe-Prater U-Bahn station.

Visas

➡ There are no entry requirements for nationals of EU countries and a handful of other European countries (including Switzerland). Citizens of Australia, the USA, Canada and New Zealand do not need visas to visit Austria for up to 90 days.

➡ Everyone else, including citizens of South Africa, needs a Schengen visa, named after the Schengen Agreement that has abolished passport controls among 26 EU countries and which has also been ratified by the non-EU governments of Iceland, Norway and Switzerland. Note that the UK and Ireland are not Schengen countries.

➡ Check www.bmeia.gv.at for the latest visa regulations and the closest embassy to your current residence.

Language

German is the national language of Austria. It belongs to the West Germanic language family and has around 100 million speakers worldwide.

In German, word stress falls mostly on the first syllable – in our pronunciation guides the stressed syllable is indicated with italics.

Note that German has polite and informal forms for 'you' (Sie and du respectively). When addressing people you don't know well, use the polite form. In this language guide, polite forms are used, unless you see (pol/inf), which indicates we've given both options. Also note that (m/f) indicates masculine and feminine forms.

To enhance your trip with a phrasebook, visit **lonelyplanet.com**. Lonely Planet iPhone phrasebooks are available through the Apple App store.

Basics

Hello.
Guten Tag.   goo·ten taak

Goodbye.
Auf   owf
Wiedersehen.   vee·der·zey·en

How are you? (pol/inf)
Wie geht es   vee gayt es
Ihnen/dir?   ee·nen/deer

Fine, thanks.
Danke, gut.   dang·ke goot

Please.
Bitte.   bi·te

Thank you.
Danke.   dang·ke

Excuse me.
Entschuldigung.   ent·shul·di·gung

Sorry.
Entschuldigung.   ent·shul·di·gung

Yes./No.
Ja./Nein.   yah/nain

Do you speak (English)?
Sprechen Sie   shpre·khen zee
Englisch?   eng·lish

I (don't) understand.
Ich verstehe   ikh fer·shtay·e
(nicht).   (nikht)

Eating & Drinking

I'm a vegetarian. (m/f)
Ich bin Vegetarier/ ikh bin ve·ge·tah·ri·er/
Vegetarierin.   ve·ge·tah·ri·e·in

Cheers!
Prost!   prawst

That was delicious!
Das war sehr   das vahr zair
lecker!   le·ker

Please bring the bill.
Die Rechnung,   dee rekh·nung
bitte.   bi·te

I'd like ...
Ich möchte ...   ikh merkh·te ...

a coffee	*einen Kaffee*	ai·nen ka·fay
a glass of wine	*ein Glas Wein*	ain glas wain
a table for two	*einen Tisch für zwei Personen*	ai·nen tish für tsvai per·zaw·nen
two beers	*zwei Bier*	tsvai beer

Shopping

I'd like to buy ...
Ich möchte ...   ikh merkh·te ...
kaufen.   kow·fen

May I look at it?
Können Sie es mir zeigen?   ker·nen zee es meer *tsai*·gen

How much is it?
Wie viel kostet das?   vee feel *kos*·tet das

That's too expensive.
Das ist zu teuer.   das ist tsoo *toy*·er

Can you lower the price?
Können Sie mit dem Preis heruntergehen?   ker·nen zee mit dem prais he·*run*·ter·gay·en

There's a mistake in the bill.
Da ist ein Fehler in der Rechnung.   dah ist ain *fay*·ler in dair *rekh*·nung

Emergencies

Help!
Hilfe!   *hil*·fe

Call a doctor!
Rufen Sie einen Arzt!   roo·fen zee *ai*·nen artst

Call the police!
Rufen Sie die Polizei!   roo·fen zee dee po·li·*tsai*

I'm lost.
Ich habe mich verirrt.   ikh *hah*·be mikh fer·*irt*

I'm ill.
Ich bin krank.   ikh bin krangk

Where's the toilet?
Wo ist die Toilette?   vo ist dee to·a·*le*·te

Time & Numbers

What time is it?
Wie spät ist es?   vee shpayt ist es

It's (10) o'clock.
Es ist (zehn) Uhr.   es ist (tsayn) oor

morning	*Morgen*	*mor*·gen
afternoon	*Nach-mittag*	*nahkh*·mi·tahk
evening	*Abend*	*ah*·bent

yesterday	*gestern*	*ges*·tern
today	*heute*	*hoy*·te
tomorrow	*morgen*	*mor*·gen

1	*eins*	ains
2	*zwei*	tsvai
3	*drei*	drai
4	*vier*	feer
5	*fünf*	fünf
6	*sechs*	zeks
7	*sieben*	zee·ben
8	*acht*	akht
9	*neun*	noyn
10	*zehn*	tsayn
100	*hundert*	*hun*·dert
1000	*tausend*	*tow*·sent

Transport & Directions

Where's ...?
Wo ist ...?   vaw ist ...

What's the address?
Wie ist die Adresse?   vee ist dee a·*dre*·se

Can you show me (on the map)?
Können Sie es mir (auf der Karte) zeigen?   ker·nen zee es meer (owf dair *kar*·te) *tsai*·gen

I want to go to ...
Ich mochte nach ... fahren.   ikh *merkh*·te nahkh ... *fah*·ren

What time does it leave?
Wann fährt es ab?   van fairt es ap

What time does it arrive?
Wann kommt es an?   van komt es an

Does it stop at ...?
Hält es in ...?   helt es in ...

I want to get off here.
Ich mochte hier aussteigen.   ikh *merkh*·te heer *ows*·shtai·gen

Behind the Scenes

Send Us Your Feedback

We love to hear from travellers – your comments help make our books better. We read every word, and we guarantee that your feedback goes straight to the authors. Visit **lonelyplanet.com/contact** to submit your updates and suggestions.

Note: We may edit, reproduce and incorporate your comments in Lonely Planet products such as guidebooks, websites and digital products, so let us know if you don't want your comments reproduced or your name acknowledged. For a copy of our privacy policy visit lonelyplanet.com/privacy.

Catherine's Thanks

Vielen Dank first and foremost to Julian, and to my co-authors Kerry Christiani and Donna Wheeler, as well as all the locals and fellow travellers in Vienna and throughout Austria for insights, information and good times. Huge thanks, too, to Destination Editors Helen Elfer and Dan Fahey, and everyone at LP. As ever, *merci encore* to my parents, brother, *belle-sœur* and *neveu*.

Acknowledgements

Cover photograph: Hundertwasserhaus, Hemis/AWL ©

This Book

This 2nd edition of Lonely Planet's *Pocket Vienna* guidebook was researched and written by Catherine Le Nevez. This guidebook was produced by the following:

Destination Editors Helen Elfer, Daniel Fahey

Product Editor Sandie Kestell

Senior Cartographer Anthony Phelan

Book Designer Gwen Cotter

Assisting Editors Andrea Dobbin, Carly Hall, Ali Lemer, Christopher Pitts, Maja Vatrić

Cover Researcher Naomi Parker

Thanks to Cheree Broughton, Jennifer Carey, Neill Coen, Katie Connelly, Daniel Corbett, Jane Grisman, Victoria Harrison, Claire Naylor, Karyn Noble, Martine Power, Angela Tinson, Tony Wheeler

Index

See also separate subindexes for:

⊗ **Eating p157**

⊖ **Drinking p157**

✪ **Entertainment p158**

⊜ **Shopping p158**

3 City Wave 138

A
accommodation 144-5
activities 138
Akademie der Bildenden Künste 84
Albertina 30
Alpengarten 98
ambulance 149
Ankeruhr 126
architecture 136
Architekturzentrum Wien 64
area codes 150
art 141
ATMs 149
Augarten 114
Augustinerkirche 30

B
Badeschiff 138
bargaining 142
bathrooms 151
beer 132
Beethoven Frieze 84
Beethoven, Ludwig van 36
bicycle travel 138, 147
Bloch-Bauer, Adele 98

Sights 000
Map Pages **000**

Botanischer Garten 101
Brahms, Johannes 36
Bruckner, Anton 36
Burggarten 125
Burgkapelle 26
Burgtheater 72, 89
bus travel 146, 147
business hours 148

C
Cathedral South Tower 42
cell phones 16, 150-1
children, travel with 140
Christkindlmärkte (Christmas markets) 74, 139
classical music 134
climate 144
coffee houses 128-9
costs 16, 148-9
credit cards 149
currency 16, 149
cycling 138, 147

D
dangers, *see* safety
Die Villa 89
disabilities, travellers with 151
discount cards 148-9
Dom- & Diözesanmuseum 42
Dominikanerkirche 127

Donauinsel 138
drinking 132-3, *see also* Drinking subindex, *individual neighbourhoods*
Dschungel Wien 65

E
electricity 149
emergencies 149
Empress Elisabeth 25, 27, 117
entertainment 134-5, *see also* Entertainment subindex, *individual neighbourhoods*
environmental issues 111
Esperantomuseum 31
equestrian shows 27
etiquette 150
events, *see* festivals & events

F
Fälschermuseum 104-5
festivals & events 139
  Donauinselfest 134
  Identities 89
  Jazz Fest Wien 134
  Regenbogen Parade 89
fire services 149
food 130-1, *see also* Eating subindex,

individual neighbourhoods
free attractions 139
Freihausviertel 80-1, **80**

G
gay travellers 89
German language 16, 152-3
Globenmuseum 31-2
Gloriette 118
Gluck, Christoph Willibald 36
government 111
Graben 53
Greene, Graham 115

H
Habsburg dynasty 24, 30, 41-2
Haus der Musik 48
Haydn, Joseph 36, 84-5
Haydnhaus 84-5
Heeresgeschichtliches Museum 104
highlights 8-11, 12-13
historic centre 38-53, **46-7**
  drinking 52
  entertainment 52-3
  food 48-52
  itineraries 39, 44-5, **44**
  shopping 53
  sights 40-3, 48
  transport 39

Hofburg 8, 24-7, **26**
Hofburg area 22-37, **28-9**
  drinking 34-5
  entertainment 35
  food 32-4
  itineraries 23
  shopping 37
  sights 24-7, 30-2
  transport 23
Hofmobiliendepot 72-3
holidays 149-50
Holocaust-Denkmal 51
Hundertwasserhaus 101

I
ice skating 138
Innere Stadt, *see historic centre*
internet access 149
Irrgarten 119
itineraries 14-15, 124-7, **125**, **126**, *see also individual neighbourhoods*

J
jazz music 134
Jewish history 48, 51
Jüdisches Museum 48
Jugendstil 107, 141

K
Kaiserappartements 25
Kaisergruft 30
Kaiserliche Schatzkammer 25
Kapuzinerkirche 30

Karlskirche 84
Karlsplatz 76-91, **82-3**
  drinking 87-9
  entertainment 89-90
  food 85-7
  itineraries 77, 80-1
  shopping 90-1
  sights 78-9, 84-5
  transport 77
Katakomben 41-2
Kindermuseum 119
Kirche am Steinhof 85
Klimt, Gustav 96, 98, 107, 141
Kronprinzengarten 119
Kunsthalle 64
KunstHausWien 104
Kunsthistorisches Museum 9, 56-61, **60**

L
language 16, 152-3
Leopold Museum 63
lesbian travellers 89
local life 12-13

M
Mahler, Gustav 36
Marionetten Theater 119-20
markets 74, 91, 100, 139
microbreweries 133
mobile phones 16, 150-1
money 16, 148-9
Monument to the Victims of Fascism 127
Morzinplatz 127
Mozart, Wolfgang Amadeus 36, 48, 117-18, 125
Mozarthaus Vienna 48
MQ Point 63
MUMOK 63-4

museum district 54-75, **70-1**
  drinking 74-5
  food 73-4
  itineraries 55, 68-9, **68**
  shopping 75
  sights 56-67, 72-3
  transport 55
Museum für Angewandte Kunst 104
Museum Judenplatz 48
Museum Moderner Kunst 63-4
MuseumsQuartier 10, 62-5, **65**
music 36, 78, 129, 134

N
Naschmarkt 91
Nationalbibliothek Prunksaal 30-1
Naturhistorisches Museum 10, 66-7
Neptunbrunnen 118
Neubau 68-9, **68**
Neue Burg Museums 27
nightlife 132-3, *see also Drinking subindex, individual neighbourhoods*

O
Oberes Belvedere 95-7
opening hours 148
opera music 134

P
Palmenhaus 121
Papyrusmuseum 31
Pestsäule 53
Peterskirche 125

Planetarium 114
police 149
politics 111
Porzellanmuseum im Augarten 114
Postsparkasse 45, 85
Prater 11, 112-15
Pratermuseum 114
public holidays 149-50
Pummerin 42

R
Rathaus 72
Regenbogen Parade 89
Richard the Lionheart 53
Riesenrad 113
Roman Ruins 118
Römer Museum 126
Ruprechtskirche 127

S
safety 150
S-Bahn travel 146, 148
Schanigärten 110
Schloss Belvedere & Gardens 11, 94-9, **96**
Schloss Belvedere area 92-111, **102-3**
  drinking 109-10
  entertainment 110-11
  food 105-6, 108-9
  itineraries 93, 100-1, **100**
  sights 94-9, 104-5
  transport 93
Schloss Schönbrunn & Gardens 11, 116-21, **119**
Schmetterlinghaus 125
Schönbrunn Tiergarten 120
Schöner Brunnen 119

Sights 000
Map Pages **000**

Schubert, Franz 36
Secession 84, 141
shopping 142, see
   also individual
   neighbourhoods,
   Shopping subindex
Silberkammer 25
Sisi 25, 27, 117
Sisi Museum 25
**Spanish Riding
   School 26-7**
**Staatsoper 10, 78-9,
   134**
**Stadtbahn
   Pavillons 85**
Stadtpark 101
Stadttempel 51
Stephansdom 9, 40-3
**Strandbad Alte
   Donau 138**
Strauss, Johann the
   Elder 36
Strauss, Johann the
   Younger 36
swimming 138

T
taxes 142
taxis 146, 147
**Technisches
   Museum 121**
telephone services
   150-1
TheaterMuseum 32
theatre 75
**Third Man Private
   Collection 115**
Third Man, The 115
time 16
tipping 16
toilets 151
top sights 8-11
tourist information 151
tours 72, 115, 137
train travel 145-6, 147-8

trams 146, 148
transport 17, 145-8

U
U-Bahn travel 146, 147-8
Unterer Prater 114
**Unteres Belvedere
   98-9**

V
vacations 149-50
Vienna Boys' Choir 26,
Vienna International
   Airport 145
Vienna Philharmonic
   89, 134
visas 16, 151

W
Wagenburg 120
walks 124-5, 126-7,
   125, 127
weather 144
websites 16, 132, 145
**Wiener Eislaufverein
   138**
Wiener Eistraum 138
Würstelprater 113
Wüstenhaus 121

Z
Zentralfriedhof 106
Zoom 64-5

⊗ **Eating**

B
Babettes 80
Beim Czaak 49
Bierhof 33
Bitzinger Würstelstand
   am Albertinaplatz
   25
Blue Mustard 32-3

C
Café Goldegg 105-6
Café Korb 50
Cafe Menta 106
Café Mozart 124

D
Die Burgermacher 74
Donuteria 50

E
Eis Greissler 86
El Burro 86-7

F
Figar 73-4
Figlmüller 50

G
Gasthaus Wild 108
Glacis Beisl 74
Gmoakeller 108
Griechenbeisl 48

H
Halle 63
Hidden Kitchen Park
   109
Hofbackstube
   Schönbrunn 121
Huth
   Gastwirtschaft 49

J
Joseph Brot 106

K
Kantine 63

L
Lingenhel 109
Lusthaus 114

M
Meierei im Stadtpark
   106
Meinl's Restaurant 33-4
Motto am Fluss 50, 52

P
Plachutta 45
Punks 131
Pure Living Bakery 117

R
Rochusmarkt 100

S
Said the Butcher to the
   Cow 86
Salon Plafond 109
Silberwirt 86
Steirereck im Stadtpark
   105
Süssi 81

T
Tempel 113
Tian 73
Tian Bistro 73
Trześniewski 33

V
Vollpension 85-6

Z
Zanoni & Zanoni 45
Zum Alten Fassl 87

⊗ **Drinking**

1516 Brewing
   Company 52

B
Barfly's Club 87

Brickmakers Pub & Kitchen 74-5

C

Café am Heumarkt 101
Café Central 34
Café Jelinek 87-8
Café Leopold 63
Café Leopold Hawelka 34
Café Rüdigerhof 87
Café Sacher 33
Café Savoy 89
Café Sperl 87
Café Zartl 100-1
Club U 88

D

Demel 33
Diglas 52

E

Esterházykeller 35

F

Felixx 89

K

Kleines Café 45

L

Le Troquet 75
Loos American Bar 34

M

Mango Bar 89

P

Palmenhaus 25

Sights 000
Map Pages **000**

Prückel 45

S

Salm Bräu 109
Sekt Comptoir 81
Siebensternbräu 75
Sperlhof 129
Strandbar Herrmann 101
Supersense 113

U

Urania 109-10

V

Vinothek W-Einkehr 44
Volksgarten ClubDiskothek 34

W

Wieden Bräu 88-9
Wieninger 133

Z

Zwölf Apostelkeller 52

😊 Entertainment

Akademietheater 111
Arnold Schönberg Center 110-11
Bundestheaterkassen 79
Burg Kino 115
Burgtheater 72, 89
Hofburg Concert Halls 35
Jazzland 52-3
Konzerthaus 110
Kursalon 111
Metro Kinokulturhaus 45
Musikverein 89
MuTh 135
Radiokulturhaus 110

Theater an der Wien 90
Vienna's English Theatre 75
Volksoper 89-90

🏬 Shopping

1130Wein 117

A

Altmann & Kühne 53

B

Beer Lovers 90
Blühendes Konfekt 90
Bonbons Anzinger 37

D

Das Möbel 68
Die Werkbank 68
Dirndlherz 75
Dorotheum 37

E

Elke Freytag 69

F

feinedinge 90
Flohmarkt 91
Fruth 81

G

Gabarage Upcycling Design 91

H

Helene 81
Henzls Ernte 81
Holzer Galerie 69

I

Ina Kent 69

J

J&L Lobmeyr Vienna 37

K

Karmelitermarkt 113

L

Lichterloh 91

M

Mein Design 91

N

Näherei Apfel 81
Naschmarkt 91

P

Park 69

R

Rathausplatz Christkindlmarkt 74
Rochusmarkt 100
Runway 53

S

Schauraum 69
Schmuckladen 69
S/GHT 69
So Austria 53
Spittelberg Christkindlmarkt 74
Steiff 37

W

Wald & Wiese 50
Wiener Konfektion 69
Wiener Rosenmanufaktur 52

Our Writers

Catherine Le Nevez

Catherine's wanderlust kicked in when she roadtripped across Europe from her Parisian base aged four, and she's been hitting the road at every opportunity since, travelling to around 60 countries and completing her Doctorate of Creative Arts in Writing, Masters in Professional Writing, and postgrad qualifications in Editing and Publishing along the way. Over the past dozen-plus years she's written scores of Lonely Planet guides and articles covering Paris, France, Europe and far beyond. Her work has also appeared in numerous online and print publications. Topping Catherine's list of travel tips is to travel without any expectations.

Contributing Writers

Kerry Christiani contributed to the Prater and Schloss Belvedere to the Canal chapters.
Donna Wheeler contributed to the Schloss Schönbrunn feature.

Published by Lonely Planet Global Limited
CRN 554153
2nd edition – May 2017
ISBN 978 1 78657 437 4
© Lonely Planet 2017   Photographs © as indicated 2017
10 9 8 7 6 5 4 3
Printed in Malaysia